BEARDED COLLIE

BACK
Level

HINDQUARTERS
Powerful and muscular

TAIL
Set low

COAT
Double with soft undercoat

FEET
Oval in shape

Title Page: Bearded Collie photographed by Isabelle Francais

Photographers: Marsha Alber, Carol Gold, Isabelle Francais, Lambie Heighton, Roy and Carla Kligfield, J. Kratz, Chris Neilson, Pets By Paulette, Sallen Beardies, Mary Jo Steger, Karen J. Taylor, Linda Teplin, Harry and Ann Witte, D. Wynen

8.28.13

To my Deseronto Friends
who share my love
for our Pets!
Elaine Lewes

Distributed in the UNITED STATES to the Pet Trade by T.F.H. Publications, Inc., 1 TFH Plaza, Neptune City, NJ 07753; on the Internet at www.tfh.com; in CANADA by Rolf C. Hagen Inc., 3225 Sartelon St., Montreal, Quebec H4R 1E8; Pet Trade by H & L Pet Supplies Inc., 27 Kingston Crescent, Kitchener, Ontario N2B 2T6; in ENGLAND by T.F.H. Publications, PO Box 74, Havant PO9 5TT; in AUSTRALIA AND THE SOUTH PACIFIC by T.F.H. (Australia), Pty. Ltd., Box 149, Brookvale 2100 N.S.W., Australia; in NEW ZEALAND by Brooklands Aquarium Ltd., 5 McGiven Drive, New Plymouth, RD1 New Zealand; in SOUTH AFRICA by Rolf C. Hagen S.A. (PTY.) LTD., P.O. Box 201199, Durban North 4016, South Africa; in JAPAN by T.F.H. Publications, Japan—Jiro Tsuda, 10-12-3 Ohjidai, Sakura, Chiba 285, Japan. Published by T.F.H. Publications, Inc.

MANUFACTURED IN THE
UNITED STATES OF AMERICA
BY T.F.H. PUBLICATIONS, INC.

BEARDED COLLIE

A COMPLETE AND RELIABLE HANDBOOK

Carol Gold

RX-141

CONTENTS

History and Origin of the Bearded Collie 7
Beardies in North America

Characteristics of the Bearded Collie 15
Exercise · Personality · Training · Unique Colors

Standards for the Bearded Collie 23
AKC Standard for the Bearded Collie · The Kennel Club
(Great Britain) Bearded Collie Breed Standard · CKC Standard
for the Bearded Collie · Interpretation of the Bearded Collie Standard

Selecting the Right Bearded Collie For You 40
Puppy or Adult? · Male or Female? · Health Checks

Your Puppy's New Home 46
On Arriving Home · Dangers in the Home · The First Night
Other Pets · Housetraining · The Early Days · Identification

Caring for Your Bearded Collie 57
Getting Ready for Your Beardie · Grooming · Feeding

Housebreaking and Training Your Bearded Collie 63
Training

Development of the Bearded Collie 68
Bouncing Into Old Age

Your Healthy Bearded Collie 78
Physical Exam · Healthy Teeth and Gums · Fighting Fleas
The Trouble with Ticks · Insects and Other Outdoor Dangers
Skin Disorders · Internal Disorders · Worms · Bloat
(Gastric Dilatation) · Vaccinations · Accidents

HISTORY AND ORIGIN OF THE BEARDED COLLIE

Although they have existed in Britain for probably more than three centuries, it is not easy to trace the history of the Bearded Collie. They were not the dog of the landowner or aristocrat; the prized possession of those who kept records. Until late in the 1940s, Beardies were mainly humble working dogs, the partners and companions of shepherds, drovers, and country folk. Valued highly by their owners, the Beardie's breeding records were a matter of local memory. Mates were chosen for working ability rather than looks, and the prowess of progeny was recorded in folk tales rather than record books. Even the name of the breed changed with time and district—Highland Collie, Mountain Collie, Hairy Mou'ed Collie. Nevertheless, enough tantalizing tidbits can be found to give us an idea of the Bearded Collie's long and honorable past.

There have been records of shaggy sheepdogs in Europe since as far back as 4000 BC. Most countries developed their own version of this sheepdog, such as the Puli, the Rumanian Sheepdog, the Russian Owtscharka, the Komondor, and the Polish Lowland Sheepdog. There is speculation that the long-coated sheepdog may have reached Britain by 2000 BC. However, we know that there was a lot of trade between Scotland and what is now Poland in the late 15th and 16th centuries, and that there are records of Polish sheepdogs being brought to Britain at that time. It is possible that these dogs, mixed with local stock, may mark the origin of the Bearded Collie.

Travel was difficult in Scotland until late in the 17th century, when roads were finally forced through the Highlands. For a long time afterward, communities remained relatively isolated from one another, and dog breeds tended to be localized. A variety of types of Beardie developed, even down to color. In some areas, the brown dogs were favored, in others, the grey. They went by different names, often according to district, such as the Peebleshire Collie. A famous book of the late 1800s, *Owd Bob,* by Alfred Ollivant, is the story of a Bearded Collie, identified as one of the "grey dogs of Kenmuir." A Beardie owner could see his dog in the description even today:

"But should you, while wandering in the wild sheep land about the twin Pikes, happen on moor or in market upon a very perfect gentle knight clothed in dark grey habit, splashed here and there with rays of moon; free by right divine of the guild of gentlemen, strenuous as a prince, lithe as a rowan, graceful as a girl, with high king-carriage, motions and manners of a fairy queen; should he have a noble breadth of brow, an air of still strength born of right confidence, all unassuming; last, and most unfailing test of all, should you look into two snow-cloud eyes, calm, wistful, inscrutable, their soft depths clothed on with eternal sadness—yearning, as is said, for the soul that is not theirs—know then, you look upon one of the line of most illustrious sheepdogs of the North."

Opposite: Curious Beardies like to use their intelligence for problem solving, such as figuring out how to open a door or unhook a latch.

Until the late 1940s, the Bearded Collie was known as a working dog and companion to shepherds in the highlands of Great Britain and Scotland.

Eventually, two distinct types emerged: the larger Border variety, which was slate grey and had a straighter coat, and the smaller, reddish-brown Highland type, whose coat was slightly wavy. They have merged in the modern Beardie so that color, coat type, and size can appear in any combination.

Two distinct types of Bearded Collie eventually emerged and they came together to form the modern Beardie.

In Scotland during the 17th and 18th centuries, there were great cattle drives from the Highlands to market and Bearded Collies were the dogs the drovers depended on. The drovers lived and slept with their dogs, which were equal partners in the drive. It was not unusual for a Beardie to race ahead of the herd to secure a crossroads and keep the cattle on the right path. At the end of the cattle or sheep drives, the drover and his dogs often had to separate when the cattle or sheep had been delivered. The drover would tie a note around the dog's neck with the dog's name and his own, and he would offer to pay for food for the dog. Then the dogs would be sent home on their own, retracing their journey and stopping at farms the drive had passed on the way down. The farmers would feed and water the dogs and let them rest until they were ready to continue on their way.

The earliest known images of Bearded Collies appeared in 1771 paintings of the Duke of Buccleigh and his dog, by Gainsborough, and of the Duke's wife and daughter and their dogs in 1772, by Reynolds. The first known written and detailed description of the breed appeared in the *Livestock Journal* in 1818. The writer summed up the breed as: "A big, rough, tousy-looking tyke." It wasn't until 1912 that Bearded Collie lovers in Edinburgh formed a breed club.

Beardies were still more a working dog than a fancier's delight, and the club quickly folded, but not before the members drew up a standard for the breed. That standard was the one accepted by the first modern Bearded Collie Club when it was formed nearly a half-century later. Written standard aside, the Bearded Collie was still a widely varying breed in the early part of the 20th century.

A Scottish lady, Mrs. Cameron-Miller of Balinluig, Perthshire, made a strong attempt to breed and standardize the Beardie as a show dog in the 1930s. Her dog, Balmacneil Jock, was a well-known show winner whose photograph appeared in a 1931 book, *About Our Dogs*, by A. Croxton-Smith. Jock was a bit stumpier and shorter-legged than present-day Beardies and his coat hung thickly over his eyes. Mrs. Cameron-Miller traveled far with her Beardies to introduce the breed, even all the way south to a major show in London (a long journey in those days), and it looked like the Beardie would finally make his way from field to fame. Unfortunately, when Mrs. Cameron-Miller died, her kennel was disbanded and the Beardie fell back into oblivion.

This 14-year-old Beardie still enjoys an outing in the woods.

Oblivion it nearly was. Sheep and cattle farming had changed. The traditional hill-herding or droving dog was needed in smaller and fewer areas of Scotland. The more obedient and steady Border Collie increased in popularity as the sheepdog's work was done in closer quarters and under the supervision of the shepherd. During the Second World War, many shepherds and farmers had to reduce the numbers of dogs they kept because it became more difficult to secure enough feed. By the end of the war, the Beardies still survived, though only in pockets where their special abilities were irreplaceable.

It was then, in the mid-1940s, that Mrs. Wendy Willison ordered a Shetland Sheepdog puppy from a Scottish farmer's agent, and, by chance, got a red-brown, energetic, bright bundle of fuzz instead that won her heart and set Beardies on the path to popularity.

The Beardie puppy that arrived mistakenly at Mrs. Willison's became the mother of the modern breed, Jeannie of Bothkennar. She had fallen into good hands. Mrs. Willison was an experienced breeder and exhibitor of Shelties and was well off financially, so she was ideally fixed to promote the resurgence of the Bearded Collie.

First, Mrs. Willison had to find another Beardie, preferably a male to mate to Jeannie. As though fate was just waiting to take a hand, Mrs. Willison found just what she wanted, walking on a beach. Along came a handsome, grey male Beardie walking with his owner who, by chance, was looking for a new home for him. This is how Bailie of Bothkennar joined Jeannie, and the Bothkennar Beardies became the primary kennel of the breed.

Jeannie of Bothkennar was the first Bearded Collie registered with The Kennel Club in England in 1948. A breed club was formed in 1955 and the old 1912 standard was adopted. The first champion, Beauty Queen of Bothkennar, Jeannie's granddaughter, earned her title in 1959. Beardies were finally an accepted breed and have never looked back. They made it to the absolute top of the heap in Britain 30 years later when a Bearded Collie bitch, Ch. Potterdale Classic of Moonhill, became Supreme Champion at the 1989 world-famous Cruft's Dog Show.

BEARDIES IN NORTH AMERICA

Although there are reports of Beardies being shown at Calgary in 1910 and exported to Canada in 1913, and in the 1920s and again in the 1950s as working dogs, it wasn't until the mid-60s that the first registered Beardies came to the continent.

In Canada, the first registered Beardie was Bracky of Bothkennar, imported in 1963 by Shetland Sheepdog breeder Muriel Ratner on the suggestion of a friend who thought she'd find a Beardie interesting—an understatement, as Muriel discovered. For the next 14 years, Bracky carefully removed any window drapes that spoiled her view and cheerfully let herself and other dog friends out of any crate or cage Muriel put her in. While Bracky was not shown—except once for exhibition at nine years of age after Beardies were recognized by the CKC—she became a well-known character among Montreal dog fanciers.

The next registered Beardie was another bitch, Ch. Wishanger Marsh Pimpernel, CD, known far and wide as Gael, who accompanied the author, Carol Gold, back to Toronto from England in 1968. It was through Gael's charm and her owner's persistence that others were persuaded to import more Beardies and to form a breed club. The Bearded Collie Club of Canada was founded in 1970, the same year that the Canadian Kennel Club granted Beardies recognition. It was also in 1970 that Ch. Wishanger Marsh Pimpernel delivered the first Canadian litter of Beardies and, shortly after CKC recognition, became the first North American Beardie champion.

In the United States, Maxine and Lawrence Levy returned home in 1966 after living in Germany and brought with them their Eur. Ch. Cannamoor Glen

With a natural instinct to herd, this little Beardie shows his talents as best he can.

Canach and Eur. Ch. Cannamoor Cardoonagh, who became parents of the first US litter in 1967. The Levys began promoting the breed in the US and their efforts resulted in a handful of fanciers forming the Bearded Collie Club of America in July, 1969. The club worked for American Kennel Club recognition, encouraging members to show their dogs in matches and, when permitted, in the Miscellaneous class. The AKC finally registered the Beardie in 1976. The first American champion was, like most of the milestone Beardies, a bitch: Ch. Brambledale Blue Bonnet, owned by Henrietta and Robert Lachman.

Since then, Beardies have grown in popularity around the world. In the show ring, Beardies are frequent competitors and winners of the Best In Show award. Beardies are also making a name for themselves in herding circles, as more owners and breeders enjoy the dogs' working heritage.

Popularity has its price, however. As Beardies become more available, they are more often the subjects of an impulse buy. With their exuberance, intelligence, and shaggy coat, Beardies need dedicated owners. "Buy in haste, regret at leisure," is all too true for unprepared Beardie buyers and as a result, the numbers of Beardies needing rehoming and rescue is increasing. Show popularity has caused breeders to select more for glamour, so the body-fitting, harsh, Beardie coat has too frequently given way to a long, silky curtain of hair that dazzles in the ring but is difficult to maintain.

However, increasing numbers and geographic diversity should greatly benefit the future of Beardies if more breeders pay attention to the dogs instead of just the show ring. There is enough variety still left in Beardies for breeders to develop distinctive (both in type and genetics) lines, instead of flocking en masse to whichever dog or kennel that is the current big winner. Since Beardies are already inbred, concentrating bloodlines will only intensify the frequency of problems and leave no relatively unrelated dogs from whom to recapture lost genes. There are already "fringe" breeders who are working to keep their dogs separate from the mainstream, but ideally, the mainstream itself would consist of a variety of Beardie "families," each a correct but individual interpretation of the standard and a source of companionship and joy for Beardie owners to come.

CHARACTERISTICS OF THE BEARDED COLLIE

Bred for companionship, Bearded Collies are lovable and make a wonderful addition to any family.

Beardies are not everyone's cup of tea. They were originally bred to be working dogs, hill herders, and drovers. Their intelligence, problem-solving ability, energy, and drive that they need for work make them interesting and sometimes challenging dogs to live with.

EXERCISE

One of the secrets of living with a Beardie lies in giving him enough exercise. Beardies have energy to spare, and when that energy isn't channeled constructively, it has to go somewhere. With the breed's brightness and curiosity, a Beardie can think up many ways in which he can use up his excess energy—and you probably won't approve of most of them!

It cannot be said emphatically enough—*Beardies need exercise!* An easy walk around the block will not suffice. Your Bearded Collie needs a chance to run off some steam. Therefore, as the ideal owner, you should plan to have at least two half-hour exercise periods with your dog every day. Exercise may consist of playing ball (many Beardies' favorite pastime), going for runs in the woods or a park, or taking long, brisk walks on a lead. Beardie puppies need more free play than controlled walks—really long walks on lead are best left until your Beardie is over six months old. Beardies love to go jogging, cross-country skiing, or join in whatever other activity their owners prefer, but this can wait about a year or so, or until the Beardie's muscles have developed enough to handle it.

PERSONALITY

Beardies need mental exercise as much as they need physical exercise. They are extremely intelli-

A playful run in the grass is just what these adorable Beardie pups need. Because of their boundless energy, Beardies need to exercise on a daily basis.

gent dogs—not merely trainable—that love solving problems. The problem may be as simple as learning to open a latch (on a crate, a gate, or a door) and letting themselves out to play, or as complicated as learning that if they can make you laugh, you'll let them get away with mischief. They are delighted when they must put their brains to work.

For instance, a new Beardie owner, who also had another breed, found her Beardie puppy happily dipping into the older dog's leftover dinner. Not wanting the pup to have the adult food, the owner picked up the bowl and put it on a nearby ironing board that was set up near the stairs. For her other breed, this would have put the food out of reach and out of mind. To the owner's astonishment, however, the Beardie looked up at the ironing board high above his head, then over at the stairs. The pup then carefully climbed the stairs to just above the ironing board, squeezed through the railings, stepped down on to the board, and contentedly resumed eating. This is the kind of thinking that Beardie owners accept as normal.

If you want a dog that will become part of the family, a Bearded Collie is the perfect choice. Here, the author sits comfortably with her two favorite friends.

For all their enthusiasm and determination, Beardies are very sensitive dogs; sensitive to the way they are handled—firm, but gentle, please—and sensitive to the emotional state of their human family. Your Beardie will bounce with you when you are feeling up, and he will stay by you when you are down. He'll do every-

thing in his power to make you feel better. It's hard to be gloomy when you have two stuffed toys, a ball, and two hairy front paws in your lap.

A Beardie that is not getting enough mental and physical exercise is a Beardie that is going to get into trouble. If you don't channel his energy into work, play, or exercise, it will go into barking, chewing, digging, and any other amusement your Beardie can think up.

Beardies want to be an integral part of the family. They want to be with their people and participate in everything they do. To a Beardie, a closed bathroom door is an affront. You can give your dog the exercise and companionship he needs, and have a lot of fun yourself, by participating in dog-related sports like obedience, agility, and herding, which is especially good for Beardies.

TRAINING

Of course, you should take your Beardie to obedience class. Make sure the class you go to stresses motivation, praise, and encouragement, not drill and punishment. Beardies are very sensitive dogs and are easily destroyed by harsh training methods. If you don't know anyone who has gone through classes or can recommend them, try to observe a few before you sign up.

Right from the moment you get him, and even before your Beardie goes to obedience class, he is

Opposite: Something up there looks interesting. Known for their intelligence and drive, Beardies need just as much mental stimulation as physical play.

It's important that you instill confidence and obedience into your Beardie from the beginning. Avoid harsh training methods; Beardies are extremely sensitive dogs.

learning things. Beardies are extraordinarily quick, so make sure he is learning what you want him to learn and not developing bad habits instead. Beardies need firm guidelines. Do not give in because he's cute—Beardies are experts at "cute." Set limits and stick to them. Otherwise, your Beardie will soon be sitting in the armchair waiting for you to fetch his slippers. He will do it with good humor, leaving you laughing at his antics.

Beardies are always testing you to see how much they can get away with. It's not always obvious to their owners that they are being tested, but the Beardie that flops on his back and plays rag doll when you say, "sit," or that leaps about like a fool when you ask him to heel is testing you. It may only take one episode of insisting that he do what you ask to convince him forever that you have passed the test.

Beardies not only learn quickly, they get bored quickly. Too much repetition and your Beardie will start thinking up variations to keep things interesting. Once your Beardie has learned an obedience exercise, keep straight practice to a minimum. Instead, train him in practical settings. Heel him along a busy street when you go for a walk or have him stay at the door when you are talking to callers. Take him into the bank or a shop and have him down-and-stay while you are being served. A Beardie can tell the difference between useful work and mere

Although Beardies are energetic and love to play, they also like to just hang out and bask in the fresh air. Allow your Beardie outside time as often as you can.

drill. He will respect work but make a mockery of pointless practice.

UNIQUE COLORS

What question about Beardies gets the longest answer? Easy. "What color is your dog?"

The answer often goes something like this: "Well, he's sort of creamy white right now, but he was chocolate brown when we got him as a puppy, and if you look at the roots of his hair you'll see that he's coming in reddish over here and sandy back there. There are patches of almost-black hair on his ears, and I guess he'll be a red-brown next year if his horoscope is right..."

No wonder people get confused.

Hard though it may be to believe, when you look around the rainbow of a show ring full of Beardies the truth is that they all started in one of four very definite colors—black, blue, brown, or fawn. At birth, a black coat is jet black; blue is any shade of steel grey, from nearly blue-black to chinchilla; brown is a deep rich color, chestnut or chocolate or liver; fawn is a dark, dusky beige. All of these colors usually come with white markings on the muzzle, chest and/or neck, feet, or legs, and on the tip of the tail. Occasionally, they also sport tan markings on the cheeks, eyebrows, on the legs where the white meets the main color, and under the tail.

It would be nice if things stayed that way. Nice, but boring, and Beardies are never boring. Those nice, solid baby-puppy colors only last a few weeks. Suddenly, you will start to notice that the puppy's coat has lighter rings around his eyes and it is lightening on the legs where the color meets the white and under the plush coat on his back. The change from black to silver, or from brown to sandy, can be gradual or surprisingly sudden. How does this happen? The entire coat begins to grow in a much lighter shade that is hidden by the darker ends. Eventually, the dark ends break off to reveal a different set of puppy clothes. This happens throughout the Beardie's life, though never quite as dramatically again.

As a Beardie grows, his coat goes through several color stages. First is that pure baby color, then the fading as the longer puppy coat grows in. The change can be so extreme that you can no longer distinguish the white markings from the colored ones. By the time some Beardies are a year old, blacks and blues can be similar to silvers, and the fawns and browns become interchangeable off-whites. At a year old, a Beardie's coat is likely the lightest it will ever be. Beardies don't like to be predictable and I've had some that stayed very dark until they were past two years old. The degree to which the coat fades bears little relation to the eventual richness of the adult coat.

Slowly—especially compared to the rate of fading—the color starts to come back. Watch for it by parting the hair along your dog's shoulders, because although the first color change in puppies starts around the eyes and legs, all future color changes first appear across the shoulders.

By the time your Beardie is two years old, you should be able to see the white markings and tell what color he is again. In the third year, most Beardies darken again to the richest shade since puppyhood. From then on, through the rest of your Beardie's life, he will give you an ever-changing fashion show, lightening and darkening as the fancy takes him.

What's the secret behind Beardie color changes? Hold an individual Beardie hair up to the light and you will see that it has bands of light and dark. The

From the time that they are born, Bearded Collies go through many different color stages. This one-year-old Beardie is at her lightest color phase.

thousands of hairs on your dog's body grow at different rates, so some are in a dark-band phase while others are producing light bands. The mixture is constantly changing, creating the Beardie's unique, multishaded coat. Occasionally, a section of hairs will be synchronized in their banding, and you will see a layer of new shade coming in. Only in that first "quick-change artistry" of puppyhood do almost all the hairs change color at the same time.

STANDARDS FOR THE BEARDED COLLIE

AKC STANDARD FOR THE BEARDED COLLIE

Characteristics—The Bearded Collie is hardy and active, with an aura of strength and agility characteristic of a real working dog. Bred for centuries as a companion and servant of man, the Bearded Collie is a devoted and intelligent member of the family. He is stable and self-confident, showing no signs of shyness or aggression. This is a natural and unspoiled breed.

General Appearance—The Bearded Collie is a medium sized dog with a medium length coat that follows the natural lines of the body and allows plenty of daylight under the body. The body is long and lean, and,

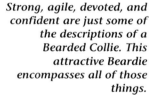

Strong, agile, devoted, and confident are just some of the descriptions of a Bearded Collie. This attractive Beardie encompasses all of those things.

though strongly made, does not appear heavy. A bright inquiring expression is a distinctive feature of the breed. The Bearded Collie should be shown in a natural stance.

Head—The head is in proportion to the size of the dog. The skull is broad and flat; the stop is moderate; the cheeks are well filled beneath the eyes; the muzzle is strong and full; the foreface is equal in length to the distance between the stop and occiput. The nose is large and squarish. A snipy muzzle is to be penalized. (See Color section for pigmentation.)

Eyes: The eyes are large, expressive, soft and affectionate, but not round nor protruding, and are set widely apart. The eyebrows are arched to the sides to frame the eyes and are long enough to blend smoothly into the coat on the sides of the head. (See Color section for eye color.)

Ears: The ears are medium sized, hanging and covered with long hair. They are set level with the eyes. When the dog is alert, the ears have a slight lift at the base.

Teeth: The teeth are strong and white, meeting in a scissors bite. Full dentition is desirable.

Neck—The neck is in proportion to the length of the body, strong and slightly arched, blending smoothly into the shoulders.

Forequarters—The shoulders are well laid back at an angle of approximately 45 degrees; a line drawn from the highest point of the shoulder blade to the forward point of articulation approximates a right angle with a line from the forward point of articulation to the point of the elbow. The tops of the shoulder blades lie in against the withers, but they slope outwards from there sufficiently to accommodate the desired spring of ribs. The legs are straight and vertical, with substantial, but not heavy, bone and are covered with shaggy hair all around. The pasterns are flexible without weakness.

Body—The body is longer than it is high in an approximate ratio of five to four, length measured from point of chest to point of buttocks, height measured at the highest point of the withers. The length of the back comes from the length of the ribcage and not that of the loin. The back is level. The ribs are well sprung from the spine but are flat at the sides. The chest is deep, reaching at least to the elbows. The loins are strong. The level back line blends smoothly into the curve of the rump. A flat croup or a steep croup is to be severely penalized.

Hindquarters—The hind legs are powerful and

muscular at the thighs with well bent stifles. The hocks are low. In normal stance, the bones below the hocks are perpendicular to the ground and parallel to each other when viewed from the rear; the hind feet fall just behind a perpendicular line from the point of buttocks when viewed from the side. The legs are covered with shaggy hair all around.

Tail: The tail is set low and is long enough for the end of the bone to reach at least the point of the hocks. It is normally carried low with an upward swirl at the tip while the dog is standing. When the dog is excited or in motion, the curve is accentuated and the tail may be raised but is never carried beyond a vertical line. The tail is covered with abundant hair.

Feet—The feet are oval in shape with the soles well padded. The toes are arched and close together, and well covered with hair including between the pads.

Coat—The coat is double with the undercoat soft, furry and close. The outercoat is flat, harsh, strong and shaggy, free from wooliness and curl, although a slight wave is permissible. The coat falls naturally to either side but must never be artificially parted. The length and density of the hair are sufficient to provide a protective coat and to enhance the shape of the dog, but not so profuse as to obscure the natural lines of the body. The dog should be shown as naturally as is consistent with good grooming but the coat must not be trimmed in any

Bright, clear eyes, a shiny, crisp coat, and a cool, wet (but not runny) nose are all signs of a healthy Bearded Collie.

way. On the head, the bridge of the nose is sparsely covered with hair which is slightly longer on the sides to cover the lips. From the cheeks, the lower lips and under the chin, the coat increases in length towards the chest, forming the typical beard. An excessively long, silky coat or one which has been trimmed in any way must be severely penalized.

Color—*Coat:* All Bearded Collies are born either black, blue, brown or fawn, with or without white markings. With maturity, the coat color may lighten, so that a born black may become any shade of gray from black to slate to silver, a born brown from chocolate to sandy. Blues and fawns also show shades from dark to light. Where white occurs, it only appears on the foreface as a blaze, on the skull, on the tip of the tail, on the chest, legs and feet and around the neck. The white hair does not grow on the body behind the shoulder nor on the face to surround the eyes. Tan markings occasionally appear and are acceptable on the eyebrows, inside the ears, on the cheeks, under the root of the tail, and on the legs where the white joins the main color.

Pigmentation: Pigmentation on the Bearded Collie follows coat color. In a born black, the eye rims, nose and lips are black, whereas in the born blue, the pigmentation

To compete in a conformation show, a Bearded Collie must adhere to the standard for the breed.

is a blue-gray color. A born brown dog has brown pigmentation and born fawns a correspondingly lighter brown. The pigmentation is completely filled in and shows no sign of spots.

Eyes: Eye color will generally tone with the coat color. In a born blue or fawn, the distinctively lighter eyes are correct and must not be penalized.

Size—The ideal height at the withers is 21-22 inches for adult dogs and 20–21 inches for adult bitches. Height over and under the ideal is to be severely penalized. The express objective of this criterion is to insure that the Bearded Collie remains a medium sized dog.

Gait—Movement is free, supple and powerful. Balance combines good reach in forequarters with strong drive in hindquarters. The back remains firm and level. The feet are lifted only enough to clear the ground, giving the impression that the dog glides along making minimum contact. Movement is lithe and flexible to enable the dog to make the sharp turns and sudden stops required of the sheepdog. When viewed from the front and rear, the front and rear legs travel in the same plane from the shoulder and hip joint to pads at all speeds. Legs remain straight, but feet move inward as speed increases until the edges of the feet converge on a center line at a fast trot.

All Bearded Collies are born either black, blue, brown, or fawn. With maturity, the coat may lighten. This one-year-old Beardie shows off her plush white coat.

Serious faults:
—snipy muzzle
—flat croup or steep croup
—excessively long, silky coat
—trimmed or sculptured coat
—height over or under the ideal
Approved August 9, 1978

THE KENNEL CLUB (GREAT BRITAIN) BEARDED COLLIE BREED STANDARD

GENERAL APPEARANCE: Lean active dog, longer than it is high in an approximate proportion of 5 to 4, measured from point of chest to point of buttock. Bitches may be slightly longer. Though strongly made, should show plenty of daylight under body and should not look too heavy. Bright, enquiring expression is a distinctive feature.

CHARACTERISTICS: Alert, lively, self-confident and active.

TEMPERAMENT: Steady, intelligent working dog, with no signs of nervousness or aggression.

HEAD & SKULL: Head in proportion to size. Skull broad, flat and square, distance between stop and occiput being equal to width between orifices of ears. Muzzle strong and equal in length to distance between stop and occiput. Whole effect being that of a dog with strength of muzzle and plenty of brain room. Moderate stop. Nose large and square, generally black but normally following coat colour in blues and browns. Nose and lips of solid colour without spots or patches. Pigmentation of lips and eye rims follows nose colour.

EYES: Toning with coat colour, set widely apart and large, soft and affectionate, not protruding.

EARS: Of medium size and drooping. When alert, ears lift at base level with, but not above top of skull, increasing apparent breadth of skull.

MOUTH: Teeth large and white. Jaws strong with a perfect, regular and complete scissor bite preferred, i.e. upper teeth closely overlapping lower teeth and set square to the jaws. Level bite tolerated but undesirable.

NECK: Moderate length, muscular and slightly arched.

FOREQUARTERS: Shoulders sloping well back, legs straight and vertical with good bone, covered with shaggy hair all round. Pasterns flexible without weakness.

BODY: Length of back comes from length of ribcage and not that of loin. Back level and ribs well sprung but not barrelled. Loin strong and chest deep, giving plenty of heart and lung room.

A Beardie's coat is his crowning glory. This male Beardie demonstrates the correct type and amount of coat.

HINDQUARTERS: Well muscled with good second thighs, well bent stifles and low hocks. Lower leg falls at right angle to ground and, in normal stance, is just behind a line vertically below point of buttocks.

FEET: Oval in shape with soles well padded. Toes arched and close together, well covered with hair, including between pads.

TAIL: Set low, without kink or twist, and long enough for end of bone to reach at least point of hock. Carried low with an upward swirl at tip whilst standing or walking, may be extended at speed. Never carried over back. Covered with abundant hair.

GAIT/MOVEMENT: Supple, smooth and long reaching, covering ground with minimum of effort.

COAT: Double with soft, furry and close undercoat. Outercoat flat, harsh, strong and shaggy, free from wooliness and curl, though slight wave permissible. Length and density of hair sufficient to provide a protective coat and to enhance shape of dog, but not enough to obscure natural lines of body. Coat must not be trimmed in any way. Bridge of nose sparsely covered with hair slightly longer on side just to cover lips. From cheeks, lower lips and under chin, coat increases on length towards chest, forming typical beard.

COLOUR: Slate grey reddish fawn, black, blue, all shades of grey, brown and sandy with or without white markings. When white occurs it appears on foreface, as a blaze on skull, on tip of tail, on chest, legs and feet and, if round the collar, roots of white hair should not extend behind shoulder. White should not appear above hocks on outside of hind legs. Slight tan markings are acceptable on eyebrows, inside ears, on cheeks, under root of tail and on legs where white joins main colour.

SIZE: Ideal height: Dogs (53–56 cms. (21–22 ins.); Bitches 51–53 cms. (20–21 ins.). Overall quality and proportions should be considered before size but excessive variations from the ideal height should be discouraged.

FAULTS: Any departure from the foregoing points should be considered a fault and the seriousness with which the fault should be regarded should be in exact proportion to its degree.

NOTE: Male animals should have two apparently normal testicles fully descended into the scrotum.

CKC STANDARD FOR THE BEARDED COLLIE

The following is the official Canadian Kennel Club breed standard.

Origin and Purpose: One of the oldest of the British herding breeds, the Bearded Collie has for centuries been the Scottish hill shepherd's dog, used to hunt and gather free-ranging sheep on the Highlands. The breed was also popular as a cattle drover. Both jobs required a hardy constitution and intelligence, initiative, strength, stamina, and speed.

General Appearance: This is a lean active dog, longer than it is high in an approximate proportion of 5:4, measured from point of chest to point of buttock. Bitches may be slightly longer. The dog, though strongly made, should show plenty of daylight under the body and should not look too heavy. A bright, inquiring expression is a distinctive feature of the breed.

Characteristics and Temperament: The Bearded Collie must be alert and self-confident, and should be lively and active. The temperament should be that of a steady, intelligent working dog and must show no signs of nervousness or aggression.

Size: Ideal height at the shoulder: dogs, 21–22 in. (53–56 cm); bitches, 20–21 in. (51–53 cm). Over-all quality and proportions should be considered before size but excessive variations from the ideal height should be discouraged.

Coat: The coat must be double with the undercoat soft, furry and close. The outer coat should be flat, harsh and strong, shaggy, free from wooliness and curl, though a slight wave is permissible. The length and density of the hair should be sufficient to provide a protective coat and to enhance the shape of the dog, but not enough to obscure the natural lines of the body. The adult coat may break along the spine, but must not be artificially parted. The coat must not be trimmed in any way. On the head, the bridge of the nose should be sparsely covered with hair which should be slightly longer on the sides just to cover the lips. From the cheeks, the lower lips and under the chin, the coat increases in length towards the chest, forming the typical beard.

Colour: Bearded Collies are born dark, pure black, brown, blue or fawn, with or without white markings. The base colours mature to any shade of black, grey, blue, brown, or fawn, with the coat usually having a mixture of many shades at once and individual hairs showing bands of light and dark. Grey hairs may be lightly interspersed with all colours. Where white occurs, it should only appear on the foreface, as a blaze on the skull, on the tip of the tail, on the chest, legs and feet and, if round the collar, the roots of the white hair should not extend behind the shoulder. White should not appear above the hocks on the outside of the hind legs. Slight tan markings are acceptable on the eyebrows, inside the ears, on the

According to the standard, a Beardie's head should be in proportion to the size of the dog. Eyes should also correlate with the color of the dog's coat.

cheeks, under the root of the tail, and on the legs where white joins the main colour.

Head: The head should be in proportion to the size of the dog. The skull is broad and flat, the distance between stop and occiput being equal to the width between the orifices of the ears. The muzzle is strong and equal in length to the distance between the stop and the occiput, the whole effect being that of a dog with strength of muzzle and plenty of brain room. The stop should be moderate. The nose is large and square. Pigmentation of nose leather, lips, and eye rims follows coat colour at birth and should be of a solid colour without spots or patches. The eyes should be set widely apart and are large, soft and affectionate, but not protruding. The eyebrows are arched up and forward but are not so long as to obscure the eyes. Eyes should tone with coat in colour. Born blues and fawns will have lighter eyes with all shades of coat than born blacks or browns. The ears are of medium size and drooping. When the dog is alert, the ears lift at the base, level with, but not above, the top of the skull, increasing the apparent breadth of the skull. The teeth are large and white, the incisors of the lower jaw fitting tightly behind those of the upper jaw. However, a level bite is acceptable. A full set of forty-two teeth is desirable.

Neck: The neck must be of a fair length, muscular, and slightly arched.

Forequarters: The shoulders should slope well back, a line drawn through the center of the shoulder blade should form a right angle (90 degrees) with the humerus. The shoulder blades at the withers should only be separated by the vertebrae but must slope outwards from there sufficiently to accommodate the desired spring of rib. The legs are straight and vertical, with good bone, and covered with shaggy hair all-round. The pasterns should be flexible without weakness.

Body: The length of the back should come from the length of the rib cage and not that of the loin. The ribs are well sprung but angled back, making the rib cage appear flat, and the chest is deep, giving plenty of heart and lung room. The back must be level and the loins should be strong. The level back blends smoothly into the curve of the rump and must not fall away in croup.

Hindquarters: The hindquarters are well muscled with good second thighs, well-bent stifles and low hocks. Below the hock, the leg falls at a right angle to the ground and, in normal stance, will be just behind a line vertically below the point of the buttock. The distance between the hocks should approximate the distance from hock to ground.

Feet: The feet are oval in shape with the soles well padded. The toes are arched and close together, well covered with hair including between the pads.

Tail: The tail is set low, without kink or twist, and is long enough for the end of the bone to reach at least the point of the hock. It is carried low with an upward swirl at the tip while standing. When the dog is excited or in motion the tail may be extended or raised, but must not be carried forward over the back.

Gait: Seen from the side, a correctly moving dog appears to flow across the ground with the minimum of effort. Movement should be supple, smooth, and long-reaching, with good driving power in the hindquarters and feet lifted just enough to clear the ground. The forelegs should track smoothly and straight. Each hind leg should move in line with the foreleg on the same side. The back should remain level and firm.

Revised: May 04, 1998

INTERPRETATION OF THE BEARDED COLLIE STANDARD

To understand the Standard of the Bearded Collie, you first have to understand what the Beardie was bred to do. Although they originally worked sheep, they were not the picture-perfect sheepdog circling a flock of sheep and driving it across a grassy plain or gentle hills in response to the shepherd's commands to move this way or that.

If that's your image of the Bearded Collie's heritage, think again. The Beardie is a hill herder and drover.

A typical Scottish Highland hill sheep's grazing area may consist of about five or six square kilometers of mountainous hillside, rising to more than 1,000 meters high. Deep ravines cut through the hills. On the lower slopes, the ravines are filled with trees and, in summer, with bracken that can grow up to three meters high. Higher up there are thick heathers and patches of marsh. As you go higher still, boulders, rocky outcrops, and cliffs abound. Go up to the 1,000-meter mark and you may find snow, even in the summer. Scattered over the area, and almost as wild as the country, are several hundred sheep.

It's the Beardie's job to go up on the hills to hunt out the sheep and start bringing them down. The shepherd can't see the sheep or his dog, so the Beardie has to work on his own. It's an exceptionally hard job. The dog has to cover the hillside repeatedly, working speedily, and he may have to do this dawn to dusk for days on end and in all kinds of weather.

The dog must be agile enough to follow the sheep across the rocks. When faced with a recalcitrant ewe, he must face her down and get her moving by himself. Problems that may arise are the dog's to solve. A hill Beardie also barks while he's working. This serves two purposes: It tells the shepherd where the dog is, but more importantly, it startles the sheep and gets them moving toward one another for safety.

The Beardie's other job was as a drover, moving cattle and, sometimes, sheep over long distances to market in the days before railways and trucks. This, too, demanded stamina, intelligence, and agility.

Keeping this in mind, let's look at the Canadian Kennel Club Standard for the Beardie Collie and the interpretation.

General Appearance

Interpretation: The Beardie's long, lean body is one of the most important features of the breed. The length provides flexibility for a dog that must change direction in a single step. It also provides the spring that adds to the Beardie's speed. Beardies, along with only a few other breeds, have a double-suspension gallop. That is, they are off the ground both when fully extended and fully collected. When they hit the ground with their legs beneath them, the uncoiling long body adds extra driving force when the legs push off again. The length of the body also gives extra lung room without increasing bulk—that's where the leanness comes in. A lean dog cuts through the air with less resistance than a wide one and is more flexible as well.

The requirement for "plenty of daylight under the body" serves two purposes. Primarily, it means that the coat should not be too long. It should follow the outline of the dog's body, not sweep the floor. Structurally, it means that the Beardie should not be short in leg. The measurement from the point of the elbow to the ground should be about the same as from the elbow to the top of the shoulder. By the way, that bright, inquiring expression is not a cute inquisitiveness, but an intelligent and questioning look.

Characteristics and Temperament

Interpretation: This is the other most important section of the standard. To work alone and to face down defiant sheep, a dog must be bold and confident. An aggressive dog working alone with livestock and other dogs would create a disaster.

Size

Interpretation: Historically, there has been a wide range of size in the breed. Larger, rangier dogs were used on the hills than on the lowlands. In fact, until 1964, the British standard called for "Dogs 20–24 inches, bitches rather less," and this was only changed because the Kennel Club felt that the range was too wide. Size alone is not that important. For instance, a heavy or fine dog of correct size is inferior to one of correct proportions and substance that is too tall or short.

Coat

Interpretation: A dog that works outside in all weather needs appropriate clothing. The coat is made up of medium-length hairs that grow in layers like a thatched roof, not of long hair that all grows full length. The thatching sheds water just like the layered feathers of a duck's back. The hairs of a harsh coat are thick, providing a watertight overcoat. They also shed dirt more easily than softer hair—anyone with a correctly coated Beardie appreciates the wonder of a mud-covered dog that self-cleans as he dries. The harsh hairs hold more oil than finer hairs, again improving the water-repellent quality.

The Beardie on the left was born brown; the Beardie on the right was born black. Coat color changes drastically with age.

Just try to get a correct-coated Beardie wet in the bath! They have little tendency to mat or tangle.

The undercoat must strike a balance between too much and too little. It should form a relatively thin layer of loosely interwoven hair that is close to the body (you should be able to find the dog's skin through it). The undercoat insulates by trapping air between the hairs. With the correct amount, the dog can stay warm and, if water does penetrate the outercoat, the undercoat will dry quickly. A thick undercoat holds the dampness against the dog's body and can take a long time to dry. Damp hair is surrounded by molecules of water where air should be—water conducts heat away from the body instead of holding it close to the skin. A correct undercoat brushes loosely with little difficulty and stays that way with minimal care. A thick undercoat easily turns into felt-like lumps that lose their insulating quality. Obviously, too little undercoat provides no insulation at all.

A note about the bridge of the nose: Though the hair is sparse, the skin reflects the color of the hair that grows from it. Dark skin grows the colored hair; pink skin grows white hair. If you look closely at your Beardie's muzzle, you will see wispy white hair growing from the pink areas.

Color

Interpretation: The description of color is clear. It should be noted that there is no preferred color, shade, or marking (within the stated limits). However, traditionalists within the breed have long favored dogs with strong color and minimal white markings. One of the unique features of the breed is the way the coat color fades from the pure dark puppy coat to the sometimes almost completely washed-out adolescent coat, only to darken again with maturity. The amount of fading is not a reliable indicator of the adult hue.

The variety and ever-changing shades of the Beardie coat can be attributed to the banding of each hair. Look closely at a Beardie hair and you will see that it grows in alternating bands of light and dark. Where the individual hair is light, it is thicker and coarser; where it is dark, it is finer. The blending of thousands of banded hairs give each Beardie his own unique color. The tan tricolor markings are deceptive. They can be quite rich and striking in a young puppy but usually fade with maturity. At adulthood, they are vaguely yellow or pinkish, looking like white hair that isn't quite clean.

Head

Interpretation: The skull should be broad enough for an adult human to flatly rest their whole hand. There should be no ridgeline down the middle. Viewed from the side, the muzzle and skull are not quite on parallel planes; the skull slopes very slightly toward the muzzle. It should never slope back away from the muzzle.

The muzzle joins the skull smoothly at the sides, with good fill under the eyes and a full lower jaw. From above, the head appears to be a very blunt wedge.

When you look at a Beardie's face, it should appear as though the nose itself was an afterthought, added like a large shiny button to the end of the muzzle. The nose leather, lips, and eye rims should always be as dark as possible and do not fade with the coat.

Eyes

Interpretation: A Beardie's eyes appear almost human in their relative position on the head. This gives the dog the best binocular vision for judging depth and distance, which is important for a dog that has to run and leap across rough, rocky ground. The phrase about eyebrows "arched up and forward but not so long as to obscure the eyes" is very important. Only the correct harsh coat will do this. A soft puppy coat, for instance, falls into the eyes. Eyebrows that fall to the sides to frame the eyes (as unfortunately called for in the US standard) are wrong. The eyebrows act as protection, keeping dirt, rain, and foliage out of the dog's eyes. Beardie eyes change shade along with the coat, so eye color always tones with coat color. There is no apparent functional reason for this but it is one of the unique features of the breed. Eyes also differ between coat colors: black Beardies have dark brown eyes; blue Beardies have grey or hazel eyes; brown Beardies have amber eyes, and fawn Beardies have golden eyes.

Ears

Interpretation: There are two basic types of Beardie ears. The more traditional ear is smaller and folded lengthwise. It tends to be more mobile than the other type, which is flat, larger, and more hound-like. In either case, it must lift to the top of the skull with alertness to assist the dog's hearing, a must for a pastoral breed.

Teeth

Interpretation: The arrangement of a Beardie's front teeth is a good clue as to whether he has a correct, strong jaw. The lower incisors should form a straight line between the lower eyeteeth. Why is a level bite acceptable? Because hill shepherds felt that a dog with a level bite would be less likely to break the skin of any sheep the dog grabbed while working.

Forequarters

Interpretation: This is the area that absorbs shock every time a front foot hits the ground. Without good forequarters, a Beardie would not last long on the hills or on the drive. The standard requirement for a 90-degree angle between the shoulder and upper arm can be misleading. Equally important is that the shoulder and the upper arm should be of the same length. This allows the front leg to travel as far forward as possible so that each stride covers the most ground and the leg meets the ground at the best angle to absorb the shock.

The pastern's slight slope, too, is a shock absorber. Too much slope and the pasterns "bottom out" with every step; too upright and they transfer even the slightest stress right up the leg.

Body

Interpretation: As explained under General Appearance, a long, lean dog cuts through the air with less resistance and is more flexible as well. To achieve this and still provide plenty of lung room, the ribcage has to be deep—to the point of the elbow—and flat. The flat ribcage increases the potential for air intake. A dog, like humans, breathes by lifting its ribs to enlarge the chest cavity, thereby lowering internal air pressure and drawing in air from outside. The greater the difference between the ribcage at rest and fully expanded, more air can be drawn in as a result. The more angled back the ribs are against the spine, the more "air room" they can create when they lift.

The loin is the area between the last rib and the pelvis. It's the connector area between body and hindquarters. In almost every case, the shorter a muscle is, the more power it can exert when it contracts. A short loin therefore provides more strength to the dog's rear assembly. The loin should be no wider than the width of four fingers.

A slightly flat croup lets the Beardie extend his hind legs almost straight back. This extension is the secret behind the Beardie's ability to spring several feet straight up from a standing start, a useful trait when working on rocky outcrops and steeply cut ravines. It shows in their typical side gait, in which hind legs drive back from the hip. A Beardie who falls away in croup cannot move his hind legs far enough back.

Hindquarters

Interpretation: The second thighs provide the power to drive the rear. They are an indication of physical maturity in a Beardie and are usually not fully developed until the dog is around three years old.

The relationship between the length of the hock and the length of the stifle is important. A hock that is too high is weak, while one that is too low does not offer a long enough lever to give sufficient drive to the rear. A good ratio of length of hock to length of stifle is about 1:2.

Feet

Interpretation: The hair between the pads is a natural protection from bruised and scratches and helps insulate the toe joints when the dog is working on cold, damp ground. It should never be trimmed away.

Though the standard doesn't mention them, Beardie toenails tend to be long (by comparison with other breeds). This adds to their gripping power when making turns and climbing or jumping on rough ground.

Tail

Interpretation: In the ideal picture of a moving Beardie, the tail streams out behind, just slightly lower than the dog's back, and wags happily as the dog moves.

Gait

Interpretation: "Flow" is the operative word in Beardie gait. A Beardie should move so smoothly and with so little wasted motion that if you saw only his topline from behind a hedge, you shouldn't be able to tell if he were moving himself or standing still on a moving walkway. When moving, a correctly made Beardie's neck and head should be thrust forward. Reach should come from the shoulder in front, and the forefeet should strike the ground at least as far forward as the dog's nose. In the rear, drive comes from the hip and the rear leg should extend fully, with the hind feet reaching well back to the buttock. There should be no hint of prancing in front nor kicking up behind when the dog is moving out. Moving away, the long stifle, combined with the narrow hips of the correct lean body, give the impression of "moving close behind." This is correct movement for a Beardie and should not be confused with cowhocking or crossing over.

SELECTING THE RIGHT BEARDED COLLIE FOR YOU

Are you the right owner for a Beardie? You should be willing to play with or walk your dog for a minimum of two lively sessions a day, and interact with him frequently at other times. This doesn't mean you have to be a stay-at-home owner. Beardies can do fine with working owners who are willing to give them plenty of time and attention outside of their business hours. You should want a dog that is a companion as well as a participating family member. You shouldn't be too proud of good housekeeping—those shaggy feet are like sponges, soaking up dirt outside and transporting it indoors.

Surprise! It's basket full of puppies. When purchasing a Bearded Collie puppy, look for cleanliness, alertness, and an energetic personality.

Don't count on a Beardie pup to sit still for more than the instant it takes for the camera shutter to click. Make sure you choose a puppy whose energy level suits your lifestyle.

You should be willing to spend an hour a week grooming your dog. You should like some excitement in your life—you'll always have it with a Beardie around.

If you think this sounds like the dog for you, you may be wondering about the best place to find one. Ideally, you should buy a dog from a breeder. When you buy from a reputable breeder, you get that person's knowledge and advice, along with the dog himself. You get the benefits of the breeder's experience in planning for and raising the litter, and you will probably also get to see the whole bunch. Beware! There's nothing more appealing than a litter of seven-week-old Beardies. They look like animated stuffed toys.

What does a healthy Beardie puppy look like? His eyes are clear and bright, with no discharge in the corners. They follow moving objects, including other puppies and your shoelaces. His nose is cool (unless he's asleep), free of discharge, and poking into everything. His ears are clean and smell sweet. He responds to a sudden loud noise, like a handclap behind him. His skin is clear and smooth, pink under the white fur, brown under brown or fawn fur, grey under black or blue fur. The fur itself is plush and feels crisp, rather like a stuffed toy. His feet are thick and springy, with toenails that are not too long.

Overall, they are clean. The tail should wag energetically, and the puppy should be alert and lively, interested in everything around him, especially people.

There are those who will tell you that the puppy who runs to you first is the one you should take. That is not necessarily so. The puppy that gets to you first is likely to be the most dominant of the litter—the one who looks for new challenges, new adventures, and who may question your authority. ("Did you really mean I can't sleep on the bed? Not even over here on the corner?") Your household may be a perfect match for that take-charge little guy, or you may prefer the Beardie pup who comes along with the crowd, but stays close to you when the others go off exploring.

Many breeders do temperament testing on their young puppies in order to classify them according to dominance, submissiveness, responsiveness, etc. They will be able to advise you on the best-matched puppy for you.

The puppy's breeder can also show you the pup's mother, the best indicator of temperament. Dad contributes, too, of course, but Mom has a lot more influence on the pups in the way she rears them. Some breeders will own the father as well and be able to introduce you. In many cases, the search for the best match leads breeders to mate their bitches to someone else's male dog. In that case, they should eagerly show you pictures of the Daddy-dog and impress you with his accomplishments.

And of course, the parents' size, coat, general build, and soundness are all good indicators of what you can expect your puppy to be like when he grows up.

PUPPY OR ADULT?

Most people want puppies because they are cute and cuddly, but puppies are also a lot of work. The cute and cuddly stage disappears in a few weeks in Beardies. The work stage stays around for months. Beardies grow fast, and their energy level and curiosity leads them into a lot of mischief as they learn house rules. They have to be housetrained, leash trained, and taught basic concepts, such as the no command, as well as more sophisticated lessons, like basic obedience. A puppy is a package of potential that will not be revealed until he has fully grown.

In an adult Beardie, a lot of the potential has been realized. He can control his bladder and bowels and has gone through the heavy shedding and matting stages of coat development. He has learned a lot about living with humans. A well-reared adult Beardie can be a delight and a joy to live with. There are a variety of good ways to find an adult Beardie.

Breeders often keep puppies "on trial" to see how they develop as possible show and breeding dogs. The breeder raises and trains the pup as her own, giving him all the socialization and experience she would want a show dog to have. Unfortunately for breeders, there's no positive way to predict how a puppy will turn out. Fortunately for Beardie buyers, most breeders have limited space and prefer to sell older puppies and adults that aren't up to show standards. As long as health and temperament are not involved, the reasons for show rejection are usually inconsequential to companion owners: The Beardie's coat may be too curly, he may be too short or too tall, his tail may be carried too high, or many other so-called faults.

Another good source for older Beardies is the Beardie rescue organizations run by national parent clubs. These volunteers take in and rehome those Beardies whose owners can no longer keep or want them. Sometimes the dog needs a new home because of family disruption like divorce, death, or relocation. Sometimes the dog has been abandoned or badly treated. The dogs are evaluated for health and temperament before being placed, and Beardie rescue coordinators try to make the best match between dog and new family.

If you do not have the time to train a puppy, adopting an adult Beardie may be the answer.

MALE OR FEMALE?

Other than anatomy and hormones, there are few differences between male and female Beardies. Females come into season and ovulate twice a year, but are not interested in sex at other times. Males are always interested in sex. Neutering can eliminate these mainly hormonal differences. Beardie males are slightly larger than females and carry a heavier coat, though spayed females carry a heavier coat than their complete sisters.

In general, Beardie males are a little softer in temperament than females. Males tend to be more affectionate, too. Beardie girls can be very self-important. However, the difference between individuals is far greater than the average difference between the sexes. So unless you're planning to show and breed your Beardie, make your selection without reference to plumbing.

HEALTH CHECKS

Like many medium and large dogs, Beardies are subject to hip dysplasia, a malformation of the hip joint that can cause arthritis and, in its most severe form, crippling. Evaluation of an X-ray is the best method of diagnosing hip dysplasia, so reputable breeders have X-rays performed on their breeding stock before

Although they are impossibly cute, puppies require an unlimited amount of time, patience, and work. Before you purchase a little bundle, educate yourself on a puppy's special needs.

mating them. Be sure to ask to see the official hip certification forms for the parents of your puppy. Hip certification is done by the Orthopedic Foundation for Animals in the United States, by the University of Guelph in Canada, and by the Kennel Club/British Veterinary Association in the United Kingdom.

Otherwise, the Bearded Collie is a fairly healthy breed. Nevertheless, you should make sure to get health and inoculation records when you buy your Beardie and you should take your new dog to a veterinarian for a health check within 48 hours. Reputable breeders will take a puppy back if that initial health check reveals a problem.

It's wise to keep a close eye on your dog's growth, size, and general appearance. If you notice anything out of the ordinary, be sure to check with the vet.

YOUR PUPPY'S NEW HOME

Before actually collecting your puppy, it is better that you purchase the basic items you will need in advance of the pup's arrival date. This allows you more opportunity to shop around and ensure you have exactly what you want rather than having to buy lesser quality in a hurry.

It is always better to collect the puppy as early in the day as possible. In most instances this will mean that the puppy has a few hours with your family before it is time to retire for his first night's sleep away from his former home.

If the breeder is local, then you may not need any form of box to place the puppy in when you bring him home. A member of the family can hold the pup in his

Travel crates are ideal when traveling with your new Bearded Collie pup. The crate provides a safe haven for a puppy.

lap—duly protected by some towels just in case the puppy becomes car sick! Be sure to advise the breeder at what time you hope to arrive for the puppy, as this will obviously influence the feeding of the pup that morning or afternoon. If you arrive early in the day, then they will likely only give the pup a light breakfast so as to reduce the risk of travel sickness.

If the trip will be of a few hours duration, you should take a travel crate with you. The crate will provide your pup with a safe place to lie down and rest during the trip. During the trip, the puppy will no doubt wish to relieve his bowels, so you will have to make a few stops. On a long journey you may need a rest yourself, and can take the opportunity to let the puppy get some fresh air. However, do not let the puppy walk where there may have been a lot of other dogs because he might pick up an infection. Also, if he relieves his

Puppies need guidance, love, and firmness from their owners in order to grow into healthy and responsible adults.

bowels at such a time, do not just leave the feces where they were dropped. This is the height of irresponsibility. It has resulted in many public parks and other places actually banning dogs. You can purchase poop-scoops from your pet shop and should have them with you whenever you are taking the dog out where he might foul a public place.

Your journey home should be made as quickly as possible. If it is a hot day, be sure the car interior is amply supplied with fresh air. It should never be too hot or too cold for the puppy. The pup must never be placed where he might be subject to a draft. If the journey requires an overnight stop at a motel, be aware that other guests will not appreciate a puppy crying half the night. You must regard the puppy as a baby and comfort him so he does not cry for long periods. The worst thing you can do is to shout at or smack him. This will mean your relationship is off to a really bad start. You wouldn't smack a baby, and your puppy is still very much just this.

Opposite: Moving into a new home is a huge adjustment for a puppy. Because they can easily become confused and disoriented, it's important to be patient and treat them gently.

ON ARRIVING HOME

By the time you arrive home the puppy may be very tired, in which case he should be taken to his sleeping area and allowed to rest. Children should not be allowed to interfere with the pup when he is sleeping. If the pup is not tired, he can be allowed to investigate his new home—but always under your close supervision. After a short look around, the puppy will no doubt appreciate a light meal and a drink of water. Do not overfeed him at his first meal because he will be in an excited state and more likely to be sick.

After the initial settling-in period, welcome visitors in moderation. For proper socialization, it's essential for the puppy to meet a variety of people—children, seniors, male, female, different sizes—early in life. However, there is the risk of infection until the puppy is fully vaccinated so you should ask visitors to remove their shoes at the door and wash their hands before touching the pup.

DANGERS IN THE HOME

Your home holds many potential dangers for a little mischievous puppy, so you must think about these in advance and be sure he is protected from them. The more obvious are as follows:

Open Fires. All open fires should be protected by a mesh screen guard so there is no danger of the pup being burned by spitting pieces of coal or wood.

Electrical Wires. Puppies just love chewing on things, so be sure that all electrical appliances are neatly hidden from view and are not left plugged in when not in use. It is not sufficient simply to turn the plug switch to the off position—pull the plug from the socket.

Open Doors. A door would seem a pretty innocuous object, yet with a strong draft it could kill or injure a puppy easily if it is slammed shut. Always ensure there is no risk of this happening. It is most likely during warm weather when you have windows or outside doors open and a sudden gust of wind blows through.

Balconies. If you live in a high-rise building, obviously the pup must be protected from falling. Be sure he cannot get through any railings on your patio, balcony, or deck.

Ponds and Pools. A garden pond or a swimming pool is a very dangerous place for a little puppy to be near. Be sure it is well screened so there is no risk of the pup falling in. It takes barely a minute for a pup—or a child—to drown.

The Kitchen. While many puppies will be kept in the kitchen, at least while they are toddlers and not able to control their bowel movements, this is a room full of danger—especially while you are cooking. When cooking, keep the puppy in a play pen or in another room where he is safely out of harm's way. Alternatively, if you have a carry box or crate, put him in this so he can still see you but is well protected.

Be aware, when using washing machines, that more than one puppy has clambered in and decided to have a nap and received a wash instead! If you leave the washing machine door open and leave the room for any reason, then be sure to check inside the machine before you close the door and switch on.

Small Children. Toddlers and small children should never be left unsupervised with puppies. In spite of such advice it is amazing just how many people not only do this but also allow children to pull and maul pups. They should be taught from the outset that a puppy is not a plaything to be dragged about the home—and they should be promptly scolded if they disobey.

Children must be shown how to lift a puppy so it is safe. Failure by you to correctly educate your children about dogs could one day result in their getting a very nasty bite or scratch. When a puppy is lifted, his

While puppies are often kept in the kitchen, it is not the safest room for a dog—especially if you are cooking. Putting your puppy in a crate or playpen when you can't supervise him keeps him from potential danger.

weight must always be supported. To lift the pup, first place your right hand under his chest. Next, secure the pup by using your left hand to hold his neck. Now you can lift him and bring him close to your chest. Never lift a pup by his ears and, while he can be lifted by the scruff of his neck where the fur is loose, there is no reason ever to do this, so don't.

Beyond the dangers already cited you may be able to think of other ones that are specific to your home—steep basement steps or the like. Go around your home and check out all potential problems—you'll be glad you did.

THE FIRST NIGHT

The first few nights a puppy spends away from his mother and littermates are quite traumatic for him. He will feel very lonely, maybe cold, and will certainly miss the heartbeat of his siblings when sleeping. To help overcome his loneliness it may help to place a clock next to his bed—one with a loud tick. This will in some way soothe him, as the clock ticks to a rhythm not dissimilar from a heart beat. A cuddly toy may also help in the first few weeks. A dim nightlight may provide some comfort to the puppy, because his eyes will not yet be fully able to see in the dark. The puppy may want to leave his bed for a drink or to relieve himself.

If the pup does whimper in the night, there are two things you should not do. One is to get up and chastise him, because he will not understand why you are shouting at him; and the other is to rush to comfort him every time he cries because he will quickly realize that if he wants you to come running all he needs to do is to holler loud enough!

By all means give your puppy some extra attention on his first night, but after this quickly refrain from so doing. The pup will cry for a while but then settle down and go to sleep. Some pups are, of course, worse than others in this respect, so you must use balanced

judgment in the matter. The best solution, if possible, is to put the puppy's crate near your bed. Dogs are pack animals and your pup will feel more secure in this new environment if he is near his new pack members.

OTHER PETS

If you have other pets in the home then the puppy must be introduced to them under careful supervision. Puppies will get on just fine with any other pets— but you must make due allowance for the respective sizes of the pets concerned, and appreciate that your

It's chow time. Good nutrition plays a very important role in a puppy's development. Check with the breeder on the proper amount and correct way to feed your new Beardie puppy.

puppy has a rather playful nature. It would be very foolish to leave him with a young rabbit. The pup will want to play and might bite the bunny and get altogether too rough with it. Kittens are more able to defend themselves from overly cheeky pups, who will get a quick scratch if they overstep the mark. The adult cat could obviously give the pup a very bad scratch, though generally cats will jump clear of pups and watch them from a suitable vantage point. Eventually they will meet at ground level where the cat will quickly hiss and box a puppy's ears. The pup will soon learn to respect an adult cat; thereafter they will probably develop into great friends as the pup matures into an adult dog.

HOUSETRAINING

Undoubtedly, the first form of training your puppy will undergo is in respect to his toilet habits. To achieve this you can housetrain directly to the outside or you can use either newspaper, or a large litter tray filled with soil or lined with newspaper. A puppy cannot control his bowels until he is a few months old, and not fully until he is an adult. Therefore you must anticipate his needs and be prepared for a few accidents. The prime times a pup will urinate and defecate are shortly after he wakes up from a sleep, shortly after he has eaten, and after he has been playing awhile. He will usually whimper and start searching the room for a suitable place. You must quickly pick him up, take him outside, or place him on the newspaper or in the litter tray. He might jump out of the box without doing anything on the first one or two occasions, but if you simply repeat the procedure every time you think he wants to relieve himself then eventually he will get the message.

When he does defecate as required, give him plenty of praise, telling him what a good puppy he is. The litter tray or newspaper must, of course, be cleaned or replaced after each use—puppies do not like using a dirty toilet any more than you do. The pup's toilet can be placed near the kitchen door and as he gets older the tray can be placed outside while the door is open. The pup will then start to use it while he is outside. From that time on, it is easy to get the pup to use a given area of the yard.

Most breeders recommend the popular alternative of crate training. Upon bringing the pup home, introduce him to his crate. The open wire crate is the best choice, placed in a restricted, draft-free area of the home. Put the pup's Nylabone® and other favorite toys in the crate along with a wool blanket or other suitable bedding. The puppy's natural cleanliness instincts prohibit him from soiling in the place where he sleeps, his crate. The puppy should be allowed to go in and out of the open crate during the day, but he should sleep in the crate at the night and at other intervals during the day. Whenever the pup is taken out of his crate, he should be brought outside (or to his newspapers) to do his business. Never use the crate as a place of punishment. You will see how quickly your pup takes to his crate, considering it as his own safe haven from the big world around him.

THE EARLY DAYS

You will no doubt be given much advice on how to bring up your puppy. This will come from dog-owning friends, neighbors, and through articles and books you may read on the subject. Some of the advice will be sound, some will be nothing short of rubbish. What you should do above all else is to keep an open mind and let common sense prevail over prejudice and worn-out ideas that have been handed down over the centuries. There is no one way that is superior to all

Sitting pretty isn't difficult for these Beardie pups because they have each other. Owning more than one puppy has its advantages.

others, no more than there is no one dog that is exactly a replica of another. Each is an individual and must always be regarded as such.

A dog never becomes disobedient, unruly, or a menace to society without the full consent of his owner. Your puppy may have many limitations, but the singular biggest limitation he is confronted with in so many instances is his owner's inability to understand his needs and how to cope with them.

IDENTIFICATION

It is a sad reflection on our society that the number of dogs and cats stolen every year runs into many thousands. To these can be added the number that get lost. If you do not want your cherished pet to be lost or stolen, then you should see that he is carrying a permanent identification number, as well as a temporary tag on his collar.

Permanent markings come in the form of tattoos placed either inside the pup's ear flap, or on the inner side of a pup's upper rear leg. The number given is then recorded with one of the national registration companies. Research laboratories will not purchase dogs carrying numbers as they realize these are

Many breeders recommend crate training, especially for owners that work during the day. It's wise to introduce the new puppy to his crate immediately following his arrival.

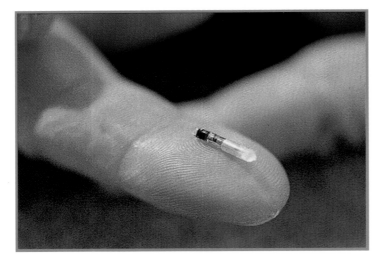

The newest method of identification is the microchip, a computer chip that is no bigger than a grain of rice, that is injected into the dog's skin.

clearly someone's pet, and not abandoned animals. As a result, thieves will normally abandon dogs so marked and this at least gives the dog a chance to be taken to the police or the dog pound, when the number can be traced and the dog reunited with its family. The only problem with this method at this time is that there are a number of registration bodies, so it is not always apparent which one the dog is registered with (as you provide the actual number). However, each registration body is aware of his competitors and will normally be happy to supply their addresses. Those holding the dog can check out which one you are with. It is not a perfect system, but until such is developed it's the best available.

Another permanent form of identification is the microchip, a computer chip that is no bigger than a grain of rice that is injected between the dog's shoulder blades. The dog feels no discomfort. The dog also receives a tag that says he is microchipped. If the dog is lost and picked up by the humane society, they can trace the owner by scanning the microchip. It is the safest form of identification.

A temporary tag takes the form of a metal or plastic disk large enough for you to place the dog's name and your phone number on it—maybe even your address as well. In virtually all places you will be required to obtain a license for your puppy. This may not become applicable until the pup is six months old, but it might apply regardless of his age. Much depends upon the state within a country, or the country itself, so check with your veterinarian if the breeder has not already advised you on this.

CARING FOR YOUR BEARDED COLLIE

GETTING READY FOR YOUR BEARDIE

Before you bring your Beardie home, you'll need to do a bit of shopping. The most important thing to buy is a dog crate. There are many types: wire and solid, collapsible and not. Choose any style that suits you, in a size that will accommodate a grown Beardie. You can always block off part of a big crate when the puppy is small. The crate will be your puppy's playpen and bed, as well as your older Beardie's sanctuary and home away from home while traveling. You don't

Food dishes are just one of the many things that you will have to buy for your puppy's homecoming.

need a fancy dog bed in the crate; puppies chew and spill. Just place a clean, washable blanket or folded towel on the floor of the crate and have some clean bedding as backup.

Your puppy will need a soft buckle collar and a light lead. Rolled leather is best for the collar, with rolled nylon a close second. You will need a soft brush and a medium comb for his puppy coat, a stronger bristle brush and a slicker brush for his adult coat.

Choose food dishes that are made of stainless steel or non-lead glazed ceramic. They should be fairly heavy, or at least able to fit in a stand that keeps them in place because Beardies love to paddle in water dishes and carry food and water bowls around, especially if they're full.

Baby gates are a good investment, especially if you don't have doors to rooms or areas that you want to keep off limits to your puppy. Beardies are born escape artists, driven by curiosity, and they will go over, under, or through obstacles that would seem impenetrable to any other breed.

GROOMING

There are many things to be aware of when it comes to grooming your Bearded Collie. Puppy coats are soft and thick and need more grooming than adult coats. The adult coat begins to come in at around two years of age. It should be straight and harsh with a soft, close (but not thick) undercoat.

Ideally, you should begin to accustom your Beardie to being groomed almost from the day you bring him home. Hold the puppy in your lap and gently brush him with a soft brush. Don't take too long, and make it enjoyable. Do this every day and gradually increase the time you spend brushing. As he grows, encourage him to lie on the floor to be brushed. If you have a table available, teach him to lie there for his grooming sessions.

By the time a full puppy coat has grown in (around six to eight months), he will be used to lying down and relaxing for the hour it can take to thoroughly brush him. Puppy coats can tangle easily and need frequent grooming. The correctly straight and harsh adult coat is a lot easier to live with and should only require a full brushing once a week.

As you begin to groom, hold each of his paws gently and feel between his toes. Lift his lips and look at his teeth. Look in his ears and lightly run your finger around the edge of the ear canal. All of this will accustom your pup to being handled, which will make your veterinarian happy and make it easier for you, too. Imagine trying to get a thorn out of a hairy foot if the dog will not let you touch him.

Equipment

What grooming equipment do you need? First of all, a good bristle brush with long, well-spaced bristles is required. Hairbrushes designed for people are great for Beardies. You will need two metal combs, one with wide-spaced teeth, the other with closely spaced teeth. These are your basic tools. It is also useful to have a slicker brush with fine, bent-wire teeth set in a rubber-padded base. Slicker brushes are wonderful for removing burrs and cleaning out the dead coat at shedding time. A mat comb is handy—it has a few widely spaced, nail-like teeth for breaking through tangles that have become matted. Finally, keep a spray bottle filled with water handy. Mist the coat lightly, section by section, as you brush—this keeps static electricity down so that the hair does not tangle and tear.

Being gentle is the key when grooming your Beardie. It also helps to have your dog lie on his side when you brush his coat.

How to Groom

It's easiest to groom with your dog lying on his side. Start by brushing a section of hair back against the

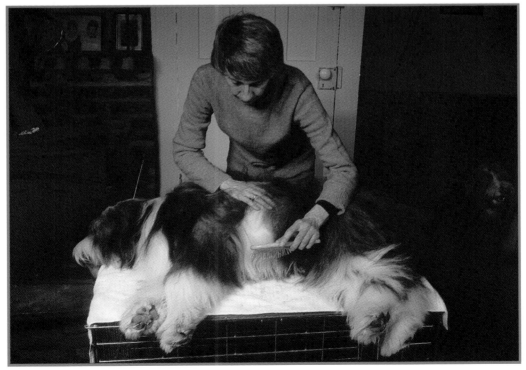

A dog and his buddy. This little guy brushes his well-behaved Beardie's coat with love and care.

grain. Use your free hand to hold the brushed section against the dog's body, and draw the hair out from under your fingers with the brush, bit by bit, as you brush it back down flat. This way you are sure to go through every bit of hair, and the light tension you place by holding it back ensures that the brush will pull out any loose or dead coat. Better on the brush than on the furniture. Work your way completely around your dog, section by section.

If you find any mats or tangles that won't brush out easily, try to undo them with your fingers. If that doesn't work, use only a tooth or two at one end of the wide-spaced comb and gently tease the mat out; start from the edge of the mat farthest from the skin and work your way in. Hold the tangled hair with your free hand, grasping it on the skin side of the mat. This keeps any unavoidable snags from pulling the dog's skin and hurting him. Try the mat comb if you have difficulty.

If all else fails, a pair of scissors might be the best tool for the job. You don't want to cut the mat out of the coat, as this leaves your Beardie looking as though moths had attacked him. You should only cut *through* the mat to loosen it; carefully cut through the mat, perpendicular to the skin. The mat should now pick out easily.

You will use the brush for most of the grooming of your Beardie. Use the combs on the feet, behind the elbows, and behind the ears. Comb out the hair around the ears and ear fringes, whiskers, and beard. The hair around the mouth should get a daily combing as well.

Beardies have soft hairs growing at the inner corner of the eye. These hairs collect matter and can grow across the eye, obscuring the dog's vision. You can gently and carefully pluck these hairs out by just grasping a few at a time between your thumb and index finger and pull. The roots of these hairs are loose and should come out easily, with no discomfort to your dog. Be careful not to pluck out too much, and only clear the hairs close to the corner of the eye by the bridge of the nose. If your Beardie acts as though you have hurt him, you've probably pulled at the wrong hairs. If you are at all unsure about this, ask your vet or groomer to help you.

The soft hair growing at the edge of the ear canal can also be plucked out. This hair can cause problems by stopping the airflow through the ear and by collecting wax. Clear only those hairs you can easily reach with your thumb and index finger. Do not go down into the ear canal and never use scissors or tweezers. If your fingers can't reach it, only your vet should.

When you're finished, let your Beardie stand and shake. (Hint: to get him to shake, blow lightly in his ear.) Make sure to brush out any missed bits and your job is done.

FEEDING

"Beardies live on air until they're two," said the exhibitor beside me at a show one day. Everyone nodded in agreement.

One of the surprising things about Beardies is how much they eat, or don't eat. For a dog of their size and energy level, they are not big eaters. Even when they are in their fast-growing puppy stage, many Beardies are just not very interested in food. They will eat a little now and then, enough to drive their owners crazy with worry and frustration, but obviously enough to grow on. Some Beardies go through phases of either eating well or being finicky. When Beardies go through the "teenage stage," between one and two years of age, they can get even more indifferent to eating, and at that stage, they often get very thin. To their owners' relief, most Beardies develop better eating habits after they start to mature, at about two years of age, although they never eat much by other breeds' standards.

When your Beardie gets to the elderly stage of his life, he may devote his life to eating, and then your worry will be keeping his weight down.

Don't panic as long as your Beardie is healthy and his eating regimen is normal (for him). Do not offer extra goodies or special treats in his dinner—he'll just learn to wait for the good stuff. Feed him a balanced diet, put it down at regular mealtimes, and pick up what he leaves after a reasonable time; half an hour or so.

Some people find success in feeding their Beardie on a free-choice basis—putting down a constant supply of dry food and letting their dog eat whenever he wants. However, if you have more than one dog, it may be difficult to control how much each one is eating, and the free-choice system only encourages your Beardie to snack.

Beardies can have sensitive digestive systems, so be prepared to try different foods to find the one your dog does best on. Give each food a fair trial—at least a month—unless your dog has an acute reaction to it, and be sure to introduce new foods gradually. Mix a little in with the old food at first, then increase the amount of new food on a daily basis and decrease the amount of the previous food until you've changed over completely.

"Should I or shouldn't I?" This mischievous Beardie has his eye on the yummy cheese and crackers.

HOUSEBREAKING AND TRAINING YOUR BEARDED COLLIE

Puppies are born with the instinct to keep their living quarters clean. Even before they can see or hear, they crawl away from their nursing area to eliminate. All you have to do to housetrain a Beardie is encourage that instinct.

Of course, the process is not as simple as it sounds.

Puppies, like babies, have a small bladder capacity and little ability to control the muscles that turn the flow on and off. Often, by the time an active puppy realizes he has to "go," he is already in the process. It is up to you to do the monitoring until growth and development solve the control problem (at about four to five months old).

Here is a way to make it relatively easy on you and your Beardie pup. First, don't let your puppy have the run of the house. Give him a dog-size den of his own. A dog crate is the best idea. Buy or borrow a dog crate before you bring your puppy home and make sure it's big enough to hold an adult Beardie. Puppies grow quickly and the crate will come in handy even when your Beardie is grown.

Set the crate up so that your pup will be out of the main traffic flow, but not isolated from the family. Put a washable rug or towel in the bottom and add a few puppy toys. This will be your puppy's playpen/bed whenever you can't keep an eye on him.

Dogs are reluctant to soil where they eat or sleep, and puppies are no exception. A crated puppy that feels the need to eliminate will make a fuss, which gives you a chance to get him outside.

Keep the crate within earshot at night. If he fusses, get the pup out quickly and you won't wake up to a mess in the morning. Help your Beardie puppy make it through the night by picking up food and water bowls a couple of hours before bedtime and taking him out just before retiring.

Puppies need to eliminate right after eating, waking, and playing. Your job is to make sure that he eliminates in the right place. A very young pup, whose waterworks have no reliable "off" setting, needs to be carried to the door when he wakes up or finishes a meal. Put him down and walk him through the door, saying, "outside," as you do, then wait with him until he performs his functions. As soon as he does, praise him exorbitantly, give him a treat, and take him back inside.

Once the puppy has relieved himself outside, let him play in a puppy-proofed area of the house under supervision. When the pup is tired (or you are), put him in his crate/den with a toy or two and close the door.

A dog crate is a good investment when housetraining your Bearded Collie. You can make the crate more appealing by putting a rug or towel on the bottom and adding a few puppy toys.

If you want to have a dog that will eventually "go" on command, you can start now. Pick a short word or phrase that won't embarrass you later. I use "hurry up." Repeat it encouragingly as the puppy looks for a spot. When you praise the done deed, use your phrase. ("Good hurry up!") By the time your puppy is housetrained, he'll know what you mean. This will surely come in handy when you are at a highway rest stop or before leaving your dog in the house for a while.

At first, it might seem that you are running outside with your pup a million times a day. Even then, if you are not watching or not fast enough, there will be accidents. What to do about them? Ignore them and assume they're your fault (they are—you weren't watching or you weren't quick enough). Use a stain remover designed for pets immediately to avoid stains or odor and pretend nothing happened. It is faster and easier to train your Beardie by praising the behavior you want rather than by punishing the behavior you do not.

As your puppy gets older, you will gradually notice that more time goes by between trips outside. This is the time to introduce your pup to the rest of the house. Under supervision, take your puppy into every room and spend some time with him. Why? This will help your puppy to form a mental map of the house, which is now his den. It often happens that a pup that seems housetrained keeps leaving solid or liquid deposits in rooms he doesn't usually enter, like the spare bedroom or a formal living room the family seldom uses. Remember that housetraining is the process of teaching your dog that the house is his den and encouraging his instinct to eliminate outside of the den. Giving him a tour of the house reinforces the idea that the entire home is the den.

By the time your puppy is four months of age, he'll have control of his bladder and bowels. So except in moments of stress (like intense game-playing), he should be fairly well housetrained. There will be backsliding, of course, particularly while his adult teeth are coming in (from about four to six months of age) and maybe again when he hits adolescence (11 to 15 months.) At those times, go back to basics—keep him in a confined area when you aren't watching him and go outside with him on "business" trips so that you can praise him for going in the right place.

TRAINING

Beardies are highly intelligent, energetic dogs. They will use that intelligence whether you knowingly

train them or not. This means that if you don't teach your Beardie the way you want him to behave, you'll have an insufferable brat on your hands.

Beardies are highly intelligent dogs, which makes the training process easier and more rewarding. This Beardie performs the down command.

Here are some guidelines for teaching your Beardie:

1. Have a sense of humor.

2. Be consistent. If you don't want a grown Beardie on the furniture, don't let your puppy up there. If you call your Beardie to come to you, make sure he comes every time, not just when he happens to be going in your direction.

3. Have a sense of humor.

4. Be firm. Beardies are very good at wheedling and at pushing the limits without seeming to do so. One way is by acting the clown. For instance, I've known several Beardies who would gaily roll over in a paw-waving, tail-wagging heap as an attempt to avoid having to sit on command. Try not to laugh and insist that he do what you've asked.

5. As soon as you acquire your puppy, start to investigate the training classes in your area. Look for a trainer who emphasizes positive reinforcement rather than punishment. Learning in a class is good for you, because you will get support and advice. It's also good for your Beardie, because he'll learn to socialize properly with other dogs and to pay attention to you

despite distractions. Classes give you motivation to practice regularly as well.

6. Have I mentioned a sense of humor?

7. Don't bore your Beardie. Beardies learn very quickly, and get bored by repetition just as fast, so keep training lessons short and varied. Use your Beardie's training in everyday life. For instance, have him sit and stay in the vestibule when you answer the door (keep him on lead until you're certain he won't dash out). Practice heeling on a busy sidewalk where your Beardie can see why he must stay by your side.

8. Give your Beardie a good play session or a run before working with him. Beardies have a lot of energy and an excess of "bounce" can get in the way of their brains. Let him run off steam before you ask him to settle down and pay attention. Then play with him again when you're finished, as a reward for good work.

9. Be flexible. Beardies think fast and if yours has figured a way around one of your lessons, find another way to teach it. Ask other Beardie owners for their novel solutions.

10. Don't lose your temper. For all their exuberance, Beardies are extremely sensitive dogs and anger is one of the best ways to destroy their trust and self-confidence. Take a deep breath or a walk around the block, and then start over.

11. And, of course, have a sense of humor. Beardies do!

Although exercise is vital for your Beardie, the proper amount of rest is also important. This Beardie isn't moving off his pillow anytime soon.

DEVELOPMENT OF THE BEARDED COLLIE

Mary, Mary, quite contrary, how does a Beardie grow?
In different ways,
All out of phase.
When he'll be done, I don't know.

A Doberman Pinscher puppy looks much like an adult Dobie seen through the wrong end of a telescope—watching him grow up is just like enlarging a picture. The same holds true for many other breeds. Nevertheless, if you take snapshots of your Beardie at eight weeks, six months, a year, eighteen months, and three years, you might have trouble convincing people that the pictures were all of the same breed, let alone of the same dog.

These pretty Beardies show off their prize-winning coats in the afternoon sun.

This two-year-old Beardie has a beautiful, healthy coat.

Beardies go through many developmental stages, and what you would expect to see in the appearance of a two-year-old Beardie would horrify you in that of a four year old. A delightful, show-winning ten-month-old can turn out to be merely mediocre at maturity, while the almost unidentifiable 18-month-old can become the epitome of the breed, given a year or two.

It is important to have an idea of the various stages Beardies go through in the process of growing up, especially if you're showing or breeding them (or even just trying to convince your relatives that the breeder didn't sell you a mutt by accident).

Every breeding family will, of course, have its own variation on development. In general, all Beardies go through most of the same stages.

Let's start with puppies. When they are between six and eight weeks old, they offer you a window on the future. What you see at that age is what you'll see when they're mature (at three years or older) no matter how ugly or beautiful they become in between. So set your puppy up and take a good look.

If your puppy has a broad and flat skull, it will probably have one at maturity. If it isn't broad and flat now, it won't be later. The stop (the indentation between the eyes) should be much more defined than in an adult and the foreface should be short and almost as wide as the skull. The jawline—the row of teeth between the lower canines—should be straight and the puppy should have a good chin. The canine teeth should meet correctly. As long as they do, then a slight overbite will probably correct itself. Some puppies at this age have narrower lower jaws than upper, and this can cause the lower canines to push into the roof of the mouth. Given time, this usually corrects itself, since the lower jaw continues to grow after the upper jaw is done. However, this can take until the dog is nearly a year old. Before gambling on a show puppy with this problem, check with the breeder about the dog's family history. The condition may be a common idiosyncrasy that corrects on its own.

Body length should be slightly shorter than you would want in an adult, although the puppy should still be longer than high. Puppies with adult proportions usually end up too long in body. Front and rear legs should be set wider apart than you would expect in an adult. The legs will come relatively closer together as the puppy grows, so if they have adult proportion there or the legs are close together at this age, your Beardie will probably be unacceptably narrow in the front and/or rear as an adult.

Watch the puppy move. His feet should track true—no turning out or in, no cow-hocking of his back legs or crossing over of his front ones. He may show all these faults later as his bones and muscles grow, but he must not show them at this stage. Even at this young age, he should move with good reach in front and plenty of drive and extension at the rear. These qualities are not going to appear later in life if they are not present at the puppy stage. This construction is hard to see in some puppies because they are too busy bouncing, pouncing, and galloping. Be patient and watch. Even the liveliest puppy will settle down into a trot for a step or two, and if you're quick, you can see what's ahead for him.

His topline should be straight and firm, no dipping or roaching his back. Tail set is important, but tail carriage at this age doesn't matter as much. Many young puppies carry their tails very high. As long as they're set on right, the tail will usually correct itself as the pup grows older.

The coat should be straight and crisp, even in its plush appearance. A soft or curly coat will never get better, only worse. Aside from being wrong, it's also a misery to take care of and groom.

Unlike some breeds, the development of a Bearded Collie is hard to predict. A Beardie puppy's appearance gives no indication of what he will look like as a full-grown adult.

By the time a Beardie puppy reaches 9 or 10 weeks of age, the window on the future has closed. The puppy grows rapidly and his various parts do not keep up with one another. Expect him to do a lot of growing until about six months of age, then slow and grow in spurts from then until 18 months or even older. A lot depends on his family. Some lines complete nearly all of their growing between six and seven months, and barely add a quarter of an inch after that. Others grow slowly but steadily after six months and can get their last half-inch or inch between one and two years old. During major growth spurts, particularly between 6 and 12 months, puppies often gain height at first in the rear, so they run downhill for a while until the front end catches up.

Front feet go off, too, and often point east-west like a ballerina's. As long as your pup starts off true—and as long as he's well-reared—his front feet will eventually straighten out, although this often occurs after he's 18 months old and is starting to gain muscle and broaden in the chest. The same happens in the rear, but rear muscling takes even longer to develop.

Along with muscle gain goes "body," a combination of muscle and bone development and padding. A six-month-old puppy should have plenty of body. There should be a nice, solid, well-packed feel to his trunk, and his ribs and hips should be well covered (but not fat). Somewhere around a year old, your nice, solid

Beardie will turn into Mr. Skin-and-Bones. Suddenly, ribs and hipbones stick out, and there doesn't seem to be a muscle anywhere in sight. You just have a sort of scrawny, gangly dog on your hands. All of this is due to the adolescent "horribles," which befall Beardies between one and two years of age. You might as well resign yourself to ignoring your Beardie's appearance for a year, waiting for time to change him back into something that you would want to show off to people.

The coat goes through adolescent stages, too, just as it does through the other phases of growing up. That plush puppy appearance you saw between six and eight weeks disappears quickly, and by three months, most Beardies look like kids who have out-grown their clothes. By six months, the first-year coat is coming in. It usually appears first across the shoulders and you can see the "break" appearing along the spine. The puppy coat is usually softer and thicker than an adult coat, but it still must have a hint of harshness and be free from curl. It often flops into the eyes. Some lines don't get very long first-year coats; others get coats of almost adult length.

After your dog is a year old (exactly *when* is influenced a lot by the time of year) his coat will change drastically. It can happen in a couple of ways. Some dogs just drop all that nice puppy hair and carry a short and scruffy coat for months. I have had Beardies that looked uncomfortably like Schnauzers at this stage. Others start to grow a new coat from their shoulders back and keep the old puppy stuff—now dry and flyaway—until the new hair replaces it. This can create a Beardie that looks like two different dogs sewn together in the middle.

Then there is color. Most Beardie coats fade to a degree. The amount of fading has no apparent relation to their actual color, to how dark they were as puppies, nor to how dark they will be as adults.

You can see the paling start around the eyes, on the legs where the color meets the white markings, or on the tail as early as seven weeks in some puppies. Others don't begin to pale until later, while some can do it quite rapidly when they are older puppies. Generally, the coat has faded the most about when the dog is around a year old. Many dogs fade so much that the white markings are indistinguishable from the colored coat. Color returns with the late adolescent coat and can come rushing back with the third-year coat (when the dog is two).

By this age, most Beardies have started to put themselves back together again, though it will still be a couple of years before you have a mature dog. By two, their coat will not be very long or full. You can tell a two-year-old by the great amount of daylight under the body. It often makes them look high on the leg. By this age, the hair is starting to arch out of their eyes.

Two-year-olds start to gain muscle and body, and you won't be embarrassed when Beardie friends drop over. Your family will even begin to believe that you have a real Beardie after all. Some two-year-old Beardies may even be of show quality. However, here is where the need for knowing a dog's age comes in. Your two-year-old will not and should not have the body, muscling, coat length, or depth of color that a four-year-old will.

Few Beardies mature in body, coat, or, especially, in mental development, until they are three or older. Most are in their prime between four and seven years of age. It is not unusual for a Beardie to be shown, and win, at ten years old.

Beardies are like fine wine—they take a long time to mature, but they are worth the wait, so hang on!

BOUNCING INTO OLD AGE

Most Beardies live to a ripe old age (14 is average) and show few signs of slowing down until they're in their

Exercise is not only necessary for the proper growth of your Beardie, but it also helps an older dog feel young. These two Beardies add a little variety to their routine with a soccer ball.

teens. From the time your Beardie is seven, it's a good idea to make regular adjustments to his lifestyle to ensure that he's fit and in good running order.

One of the easiest and most important adjustments you can make is in his diet. An older dog needs fewer calories than a younger one. Even if your Beardie weighs the same as he always did, his body composition changes. In older dogs, as in older people, muscle tissue tends give way to fat. You can feel the change in muscling on an older Beardie by feeling his outer thigh. What used to be a nicely rounded muscle bulge is, in an old dog, rather sunken. Therefore, an older dog should weigh less than he did in his prime.

You'll know your Beardie is about the right weight when you can feel his ribs without prodding and there's no layer of fat covering his shoulders. Be careful—fat distribution changes in the older dog, so you may be able to feel his backbone while a carload of fat hangs underneath. When in doubt, check with your veterinarian.

Exercise

Exercise keeps life in the old dog, so make sure that your older Beardie gets enough physical activity. You won't notice much change in your Beardie's bounce until he's ten or more, and even then, you may have to compare him to a young dog in order to spot the differences.

If your dog is obedience trained, running through the basic exercises is good for his muscles, bones, and brains. Don't think an old Beardie can't learn new tricks—they'll love the challenge and the attention.

Games may have to change as your Beardie ages. For instance, retrieving a ball becomes difficult as his

An older Beardie's coat tends to soften and tangle more easily. Make sure you know how to properly groom your Beardie at all stages of his life.

Although most dogs need time to get used to the routine, nail clipping is an absolute must in the grooming process.

eyesight dims. Try brightly colored balls that contrast with the surroundings. Roll the ball instead of throwing it, since it is easier for an old dog to follow and they don't have to stop so suddenly to grab it. Have fun with your older dog, but don't push him too much. Let him set his own pace.

Grooming

The coat softens in older Beardies and tangles more easily. It also grows to great lengths, but doesn't stay stuck into the skin as well as it had before. There's always loose hair that turns tangles into mats. To make matters (and mats) worse, old Beardies have very sensitive skin and brushing can be very uncomfortable for them. Change to a softer brush or use a slicker and groom more frequently, but for shorter periods.

Consider trimming the coat of your old Beardie short, but not shaving him. That would expose him to heat and cold, sun and rain. Just trim the coat down to an inch or two all over. It's easier to groom and doesn't mat as much. A trimmed coat doesn't collect so many leaves, twigs, or snow. Soft coats absorb much more water than hard coats. If your old Beardie gets wet, a long coat will take quite a while to dry and dampness is not good for old dogs. Trimming the coat will make him look like a puppy and feel more like one, too.

Old nails are thicker and harder, and because your old Beardie is less active, the nails don't wear down as much. Check them more frequently and keep them clipped.

Elimination

In many ways, life is a circle and you'll face some of the same problems in your old dog as you did in his puppyhood. One of them is bladder control. Old dogs can't "hold it" as long as they used to. When you have to leave him for a while, confine him to an area that won't be damaged if he springs a leak. Keep it covered with newspapers. And don't scold an old dog who has an accident—old dogs are usually upset and embarrassed about soiling their den.

One problem with older bitches—particularly spayed bitches—is that as hormone production decreases, the muscle that controls the bladder opening loses tone. The bladder never closes tightly and the bitch dribbles urine. There are a variety of medications (including hormone supplements) that will treat this problem. Consult your vet.

Sight and Hearing

You may not notice immediately that your Beardie doesn't see or hear as well as he used to. He might be able to find a thrown ball perfectly well, but not be able to see you throw it. He might be able to see a moving squirrel across the street on a sunny day, but bump into moved furniture in a lamp-lit room. It's only sensible to avoid moving things in an old dog's environment or to walk him around the new layout if you must shift things. Don't leave stairwell doors open if they're normally closed. Most dogs adjust to the changes of age.

Some older dogs experience minor balance problems as their eyesight dims. For instance, your old Beardie may not be able to judge his position as he leans over to get a drink of water and might perform a nose-dive right into the bowl. If your dog seems to lose his balance severely or frequently, consult your vet.

You'll probably notice your Beardie's inevitable hearing loss when you realize you have to shout to wake him. Be careful about touching him by surprise. Since he doesn't hear as well, he may not be aware of your approach and is more easily startled. Startled dogs may instinctively snap first and ask questions later. Put your hand in front of his nose and let him smell you before touching him. Old Beardies that are hard of hearing often fall into the habit of monotonous barking. Often, they don't seem to realize they're doing it, and you have to get their attention to stop them. Sometimes, it's as though they're talking to themselves. One of my old Beardies used to face into a corner and just bark away.

Don't take your old Beardie for off-lead walks. He cannot see danger as well and he cannot hear your calls. If you stand still and quiet, he may lose you and panic. The lead gives him security and safety.

Emotions

Being old doesn't mean being left out. Your old Beardie may no longer be able to keep up on the long hikes or cross-country ski trails, but he still needs to feel that he is part of the family. Make an effort to give him extra attention, especially if there are younger dogs in the house. Play a special game with the older dog alone. Give him a chance to show how well he remembers his obedience lessons and tricks. If he has trouble with walks, let him be the dog who accompanies you in the car.

What about adding a puppy to the household? It's a great idea to do it before your older Beardie really shows his age. Many 10- or 11-year-old Beardies get a whole new lease on life when a puppy arrives. Just be sure to give your older dog extra attention to avoid his feeling pushed aside. If your dog is much older than 11 or noticeably slowing down, it may be kinder to him, as well as easier on you, to wait until he's gone before getting a new pup.

Health

Take your old Beardie to the vet for his annual shots and a thorough physical. Watch for any sudden changes in his behavior, eating, or elimination. When you groom, check for sores or lumps under the skin. In all cases, check with your veterinarian.

The End

It will come too soon. Let yourself mourn your lost friend. Too often, society discounts the grief we feel for our departed pets. Your emotions are valid and need to be expressed. Many veterinarians can refer you to grief counseling specifically for pet owners.

What to do with the empty shell your Beardie left behind? The best place to keep your departed Beardie is in your memory, and don't ever expect to have another exactly like him.

YOUR HEALTHY BEARDED COLLIE

Dogs, like all other animals, are capable of contracting problems and diseases that, in most cases, are easily avoided by sound husbandry—meaning well-bred and well-cared-for animals are less prone to developing diseases and problems than are carelessly bred and neglected animals. Your knowledge of how to avoid problems is far more valuable than all of the books and advice on how to cure them. Respectively, the only person you should listen to about treatment is your vet. Veterinarians don't have all the answers, but at least they are trained to analyze and treat illnesses, and are aware of the full implications of treatments. This does not mean a few old remedies aren't good standbys when all else fails, but in most cases modern science provides the best treatments for disease.

Opposite: As a responsible Bearded Collie owner, you should have a basic understanding of the medical problems that affect the breed.

PHYSICAL EXAMS

Your puppy should receive regular physical examinations or check-ups. These come in two forms. One is obviously performed by your vet, and the other is a day-to-day procedure that should be done by you. Apart from the fact the exam will highlight any problem at an early stage, it is an excellent way of socializing the pup to being handled.

To do the physical exam yourself, start at the head and work your way around the body. You are looking for any sign of lesions, or any indication of parasites on the pup. The most common parasites are fleas and ticks.

A thorough oral exam should be part of your Bearded Collie's veterinary check-up.

HEALTHY TEETH AND GUMS

Chewing is instinctual. Puppies chew so that their teeth and jaws grow strong and healthy as they develop. As the permanent teeth begin to emerge, it is painful and annoying to the puppy, and puppy owners must recognize that their new charges need something safe upon which to chew. Unfortunately, once the puppy's permanent teeth have emerged and settled solidly into the jaw, the chewing instinct does not fade. Adult dogs instinctively need to clean their teeth, massage their gums, and exercise their jaws through chewing.

It is necessary for your dog to have clean teeth. You should take your dog to the veterinarian at least once a year to have his teeth cleaned and to have his mouth examined for any sign of oral disease. Although dogs do not get cavities in the same way humans do, dogs'

The Hercules® by Nylabone® has raised dental tips that help fight plaque on your Bearded Collie's teeth and gums.

teeth accumulate tartar, and more quickly than humans do! Veterinarians recommend brushing your dog's teeth daily. But who can find time to brush their dog's teeth daily? The accumulation of tartar and plaque on our dog's teeth when not removed can cause irritation and eventually erode the enamel and finally destroy the teeth. Advanced cases, while destroying the teeth, bring on gingivitis and periodontitis, two very serious conditions that can affect the dog's internal organs as well...to say nothing about bad breath!

Raised dental tips on the surface of every Plaque Attacker™ help to combat plaque and tartar.

Since everyone can't brush their dog's teeth daily or get to the veterinarian often enough for him to scale

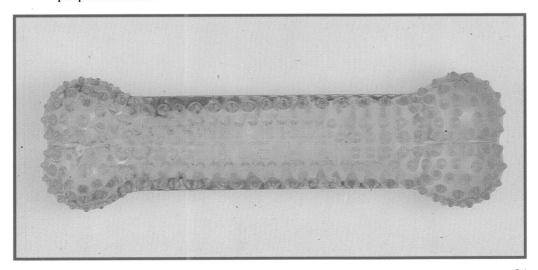

the dog's teeth, providing the dog with something safe to chew on will help maintain oral hygeine. Chew devices from Nylabone® keep dogs' teeth clean, but they also provide an excellent resource for entertainment and relief of doggie tensions. Nylabone® products give your dog something to do for an hour or two every day and during that hour or two, your dog will be taking an active part in keeping his teeth and gums healthy…without even realizing it! That's invaluable to your dog, and valuable to you!

Nylabone® provides fun bones, challenging bones, and *safe* bones. It is an owner's responsibility to recognize safe chew toys from dangerous ones. Your dog will chew and devour anything you give him. Dogs must not be permitted to chew on items that they can break. Pieces of broken objects can do internal damage to a dog, besides ripping the dog's mouth. Cheap plastic or rubber toys can cause stoppage in the intestines; such stoppages are operable only if caught immediately.

The most obvious choices, in this case, may be the worst choice. Natural beef bones were not designed for chewing and cannot take too much pressure from the sides. Due to the abrasive nature of these bones, they should be offered most sparingly. Knuckle bones, though once very popular for dogs, can be easily

Nylabone® is the only plastic dog bone made of 100% virgin nylon, specially processed to create a tough, durable, completely safe bone.

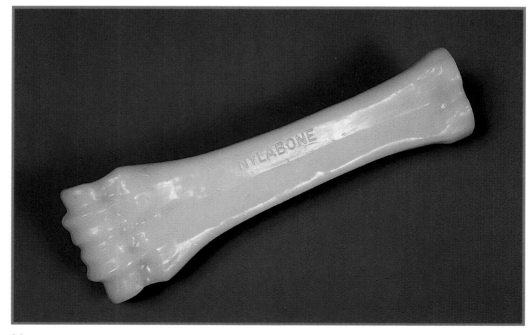

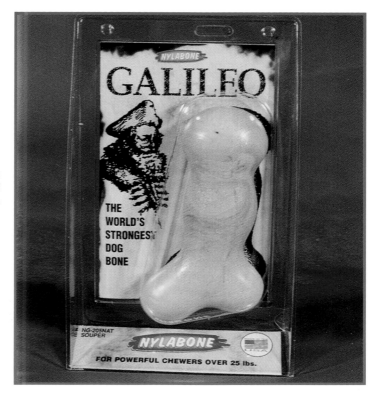

The Galileo™ is flavored to appeal to your dog and annealed so it has a relatively soft outer layer.

chewed up and eaten by dogs. At the very least, digestion is interrupted; at worst, the dog can choke or suffer from intestinal blockage.

When a dog chews hard on a Nylabone®, little bristle-like projections appear on the surface of the bone. These help to clean the dog's teeth and add to the gum-massaging. Given the chemistry of the nylon, the bristle can pass through the dog's intestinal tract without effect. Since nylon is inert, no micro-organism can grow on it, and it can be washed in soap and water or sterilized in boiling water or in an autoclave.

For the sake of your dog, his teeth and your own peace of mind, provide your dog with Nylabones®. They have 100 variations from which to choose.

FIGHTING FLEAS

Fleas are very mobile and may be red, black, or brown in color. The adults suck the blood of the host, while the larvae feed on the feces of the adults, which is rich in blood. Flea "dirt" may be seen on the pup as very tiny clusters of blackish specks that look like freshly ground pepper. The eggs of fleas may be laid on the puppy, though they are more commonly laid off the host in a favorable place, such as the bedding. They normally hatch in 4 to 21 days, depending on the temperature, but they can survive for up to 18 months if temperature conditions are not favorable. The larvae are maggot-like and molt a couple of times before forming pupae, which can survive long periods until the temperature, or the vibration of a nearby host, causes them to emerge and jump on a host.

There are a number of effective treatments available, and you should discuss them with your veterinarian, then follow all instructions for the one you choose. Any treatment will involve a product for your puppy or dog and one for the environment, and will require diligence on your part to treat all areas and thoroughly clean your home and yard until the infestation is eradicated.

THE TROUBLE WITH TICKS

Ticks are arthropods of the spider family, which means they have eight legs (though the larvae have six). They bury their headparts into the host and gorge on its blood. They are easily seen as small grain-like creatures sticking out from the skin. They are often picked up when dogs play in fields, but may also arrive in your yard via wild animals—even birds—or stray cats and dogs. Some ticks are species-specific, others are more adaptable and will host on many species.

The cat flea is the most common flea of dogs. It starts feeding soon after it makes contact with the dog.

The deer tick is the most common carrier of Lyme disease. Photo courtesy of Virbac Laboratories, Inc., Fort Worth, Texas.

The most troublesome type of tick is the deer tick, which spreads the deadly Lyme disease that can cripple a dog (or a person). Deer ticks are tiny and very hard to detect. Often, by the time they're big enough to notice, they've been feeding on the dog for a few days—long enough to do their damage. Lyme disease was named for the area of the United States in which it was first detected—Lyme, Connecticut—but has now been diagnosed in almost all parts of the U.S. Your veterinarian can advise you of the danger to your dog(s) in your area, and may suggest your dog be vaccinated for Lyme. Always go over your dog with a fine-toothed flea comb when you come in from walking through any area that may harbor deer ticks, and if your dog is acting unusually sluggish or sore, seek veterinary advice.

Attempts to pull a tick free will invariably leave the headpart in the pup, where it will die and cause an infected wound or abscess. The best way to remove ticks is to dab a strong saline solution, iodine, or alcohol on them. This will numb them, causing them to loosen their hold, at which time they can be removed with forceps. The wound can then be cleaned and covered with an antiseptic ointment. If ticks are common in your area, consult with your vet for a suitable pesticide to be used in kennels, on bedding, and on the puppy or dog.

INSECTS AND OTHER OUTDOOR DANGERS

There are many biting insects, such as mosquitoes, that can cause discomfort to a puppy. Many diseases are transmitted by the males of these species.

A pup can easily get a grass seed or thorn lodged between his pads or in the folds of his ears. These may go unnoticed until an abscess forms.

This is where your daily check of the puppy or dog will do a world of good. If your puppy has been playing in long grass or places where there may be thorns, pine needles, wild animals, or parasites, the check-up is a wise precaution.

There are many parasites such as fleas and ticks, that your dog can encounter, so closely supervise him when he is outside.

SKIN DISORDERS

Apart from problems associated with lesions created by biting pests, a puppy may fall foul to a number of other skin disorders. Examples are ringworm, mange, and eczema. Ringworm is not caused by a worm, but is a fungal infection. It manifests itself as a sore-looking bald circle. If your puppy should have any form of bald patches, let your veterinarian check him over; a microscopic examination can confirm the condition. Many old remedies for ringworm exist, such as iodine, carbolic acid, formalin, and other tinctures, but modern drugs are superior.

Fungal infections can be very difficult to treat, and even more difficult to eradicate, because of the spores. These can withstand most treatments, other than burning, which is the best thing to do with bedding once the condition has been confirmed.

Mange is a general term that can be applied to many skin conditions where the hair falls out and a flaky crust develops and falls away.

Often, dogs will scratch themselves, and this invariably is worse than the original condition, for it opens lesions that are then subject to viral, fungal, or parasitic attack. The cause of the problem can be various species of mites. These either live on skin debris and the hair follicles, which they destroy, or they bury themselves just beneath the skin and feed on the tissue. Applying general remedies from pet stores is not recommended because it is essential to identify the type of mange before a specific treatment is effective.

Eczema is another non-specific term applied to many skin disorders. The condition can be brought about in many ways. Sunburn, chemicals, allergies to foods, drugs, pollens, and even stress can all produce a deterioration of the skin and coat. Given the range of causal factors, treatment can be difficult because the problem is one of identification. It is a case of taking each possibility at a time and trying to correctly diagnose the matter. If the cause is of a dietary nature then you must remove one item at a time in order to find out if the dog is allergic to a given food. It could, of course, be the lack of a nutrient that is the problem, so if the condition persists, you should consult your veterinarian.

INTERNAL DISORDERS

It cannot be overstressed that it is very foolish to attempt to diagnose an internal disorder without the advice of a veterinarian. Take a relatively common problem such as diarrhea. It might be caused by nothing more serious than the puppy hogging a lot of food or eating something that it has never previously eaten. Conversely, it could be the first indication of a potentially fatal disease. It's up to your veterinarian to make the correct diagnosis.

The following symptoms, especially if they accompany each other or are progressively added to earlier symptoms, mean you should visit the veterinarian right away:

Continual vomiting. All dogs vomit from time to time and this is not necessarily a sign of illness. They will eat grass to induce vomiting. It is a natural cleansing process common to many carnivores. However, continued vomiting is a clear sign of a problem. It may be a blockage in the pup's intestinal tract, it may be induced by worms, or it could be due to any number of diseases.

Diarrhea. This, too, may be nothing more than a temporary condition due to many factors. Even a change of home can induce diarrhea, because this often stresses the pup, and invariably there is some change in the diet. If it persists more than 48 hours then something is amiss. If blood is seen in the feces, waste no time at all in taking the dog to the vet.

Running eyes and/or nose. A pup might have a chill and this will cause the eyes and nose to weep. Again, this should quickly clear up if the puppy is placed in a warm environment and away from any drafts. If it does not, and especially if a mucous discharge is seen, then the pup has an illness that must be diagnosed.

Coughing. Prolonged coughing is a sign of a problem, usually of a respiratory nature.

Wheezing. If the pup has difficulty breathing and makes a wheezing sound when breathing, then something is wrong.

Cries when attempting to defecate or urinate. This might only be a minor problem due to the hard state of the feces, but it could be more serious, especially if the pup cries when urinating.

Cries when touched. Obviously, if you do not handle a puppy with care he might yelp. However, if he cries even when lifted gently, then he has an internal problem that becomes apparent when pressure is applied to a given area of the body. Clearly, this must be diagnosed.

Refuses food. Generally, puppies and dogs are greedy creatures when it comes to feeding time. Some might be more fussy, but none should refuse more than one meal. If they go for a number of hours without showing any interest in their food, then something is not as it should be.

General listlessness. All puppies have their off days when they do not seem their usual cheeky, mischievous selves. If this condition persists for more than two days then there is little doubt of a problem. They may not show any of the signs listed, other than perhaps a reduced interest in their food. There are many diseases that can develop internally without displaying obvious clinical signs. Blood, fecal, and other tests are needed in order to identify the disorder before it reaches an advanced state that may not be treatable.

WORMS

There are many species of worms, and a number of these live in the tissues of dogs and most other animals. Many create no problem at all, so you are not even aware they exist. Others can be tolerated in small levels, but become a major problem if they number more than a few. The most common types seen in dogs are roundworms and tapeworms. While roundworms are the greater problem, tapeworms require an intermediate host so are more easily eradicated.

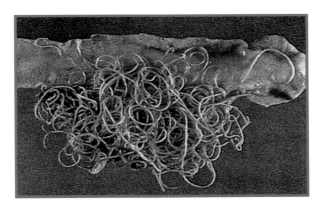

Roundworms are spaghetti-like worms that cause a pot-bellied appearance and dull coat, along with more severe symptoms, such as diarrhea and vomiting. Photo courtesy of Merck AgVet.

Roundworms of the species *Toxocara canis* infest the dog. They may grow to a length of 8 inches (20 cm) and look like strings of spaghetti. The worms feed on the digesting food in the pup's intestines. In chronic cases the puppy will become pot-bellied, have diarrhea, and will vomit. Eventually, he will stop eating, having passed through the stage when he always seems hungry. The worms lay eggs in the puppy and these pass out in his feces. They are then either ingested by the pup, or they are eaten by mice, rats, or beetles. These may then be eaten by the puppy and the life cycle is complete.

Larval worms can migrate to the womb of a pregnant bitch, or to her mammary glands, and this is how they pass to the puppy. The pregnant bitch can be wormed, which will help. The pups can, and should,

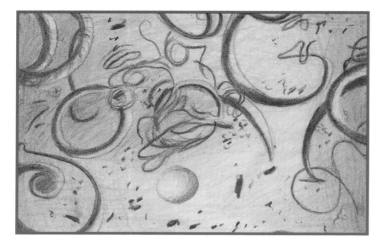

Whipworms are hard to find unless you strain your dog's feces, and this is best left to a veterinarian. Pictured here are adult whipworms.

be wormed when they are about two weeks old. Repeat worming every 10 to 14 days and the parasites should be removed. Worms can be extremely dangerous to young puppies, so you should be sure the pup is wormed as a matter of routine.

Tapeworms can be seen as tiny rice-like eggs sticking to the puppy's or dog's anus. They are less destructive, but still undesirable. The eggs are eaten by mice, fleas, rabbits, and other animals that serve as intermediate hosts. They develop into a larval stage and the host must be eaten by the dog in order to complete the chain. Your vet will supply a suitable remedy if tapeworms are seen or suspected. There are other worms, such as hookworms and whipworms, that are also blood suckers. They will make a pup anemic, and blood might be seen in the feces, which can be examined by the vet to confirm their presence. Cleanliness in all matters is the best preventative measure for all worms.

Heartworm infestation in dogs is passed by mosquitoes but can be prevented by a monthly (or daily) treatment that is given orally. Talk to your vet about the risk of heartworm in your area.

BLOAT (GASTRIC DILATATION)

This condition has proved fatal in many dogs, especially large and deep-chested breeds, such as the Weimaraner and the Great Dane. However, any dog can get bloat. It is caused by swallowing air during exercise, food/water gulping or another strenuous task. As many believe, it is not the result of flatulence. The stomach of an affected dog twists, disallowing food and blood flow and resulting in harmful toxins being released into the bloodstream. Death can easily follow if the condition goes undetected.

The best preventative measure is not to feed large meals or exercise your puppy or dog immediately after he has eaten. Veterinarians recommend feeding three smaller meals per day in an elevated feeding rack, adding water to dry food to prevent gulping, and not offering water during mealtimes.

VACCINATIONS

Every puppy, purebred or mixed breed, should be vaccinated against the major canine diseases. These are distemper, leptospirosis, hepatitis, and canine parvovirus. Your puppy may have received a temporary vaccination against distemper before you purchased him, but be sure to ask the breeder to be sure.

The age at which vaccinations are given can vary, but will usually be when the pup is 8 to 12 weeks old. By this time any protection given to the pup by antibodies received from his mother via her initial milk feeds will be losing their strength.

The puppy's immune system works on the basis that the white blood cells engulf and render harmless

Rely on your veterinarian for the most effectual vaccination schedule for your Bearded Collie puppy.

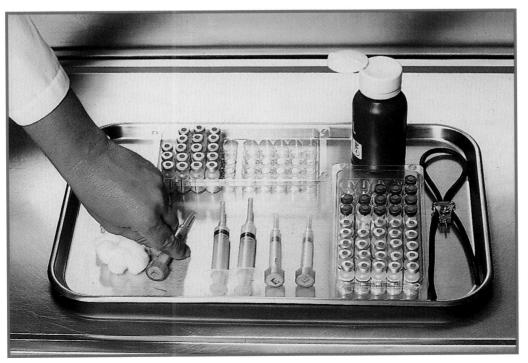

attacking bacteria. However, they must first recognize a potential enemy.

Vaccines are either dead bacteria or they are live, but in very small doses. Either type prompts the pup's defense system to attack them. When a large attack then comes (if it does), the immune system recognizes it and massive numbers of lymphocytes (white blood corpuscles) are mobilized to counter the attack. However, the ability of the cells to recognize these dangerous viruses can diminish over a period of time. It is therefore useful to provide annual reminders about the nature of the enemy. This is done by means of booster injections that keep the immune system on its alert. Immunization is not 100-percent guaranteed to be successful, but is very close. Certainly it is better than giving the puppy no protection.

Dogs are subject to other viral attacks, and if these are of a high-risk factor in your area, then your vet will suggest you have the puppy vaccinated against these as well.

Your puppy or dog should also be vaccinated against the deadly rabies virus. In fact, in many places it is illegal for your dog not to be vaccinated. This is to protect your dog, your family, and the rest of the animal population from this deadly virus that infects the nervous system and causes dementia and death.

ACCIDENTS

All puppies will get their share of bumps and bruises due to the rather energetic way they play. These will usually heal themselves over a few days. Small cuts should be bathed with a suitable disinfectant and then smeared with an antiseptic ointment. If a cut looks more serious, then stem the flow of blood with a towel or makeshift tourniquet and rush the pup to the veterinarian. Never apply so much pressure to the wound that it might restrict the flow of blood to the limb.

In the case of burns you should apply cold water or an ice pack to the surface. If the burn was due to a chemical, then this must be washed away with copious amounts of water. Apply petroleum jelly, or any vegetable oil, to the burn. Trim away the hair if need be. Wrap the dog in a blanket and rush him to the vet. The pup may go into shock, depending on the severity of the burn, and this will result in a lowered blood pressure, which is dangerous and the reason the pup must receive immediate veterinary attention.

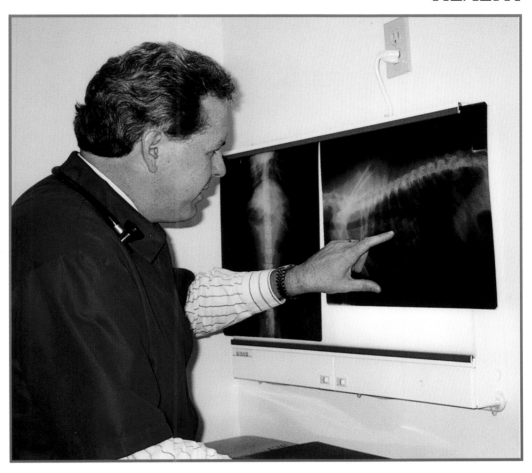

It is a good idea to x-ray the chest and abdomen on any dog hit by a car.

If a broken limb is suspected then try to keep the animal as still as possible. Wrap your pup or dog in a blanket to restrict movement and get him to the veterinarian as soon as possible. Do not move the dog's head so it is tilting backward, as this might result in blood entering the lungs.

Do not let your pup jump up and down from heights, as this can cause considerable shock to the joints. Like all youngsters, puppies do not know when enough is enough, so you must do all their thinking for them.

Provided you apply strict hygiene to all aspects of raising your puppy, and you make daily checks on his physical state, you have done as much as you can to safeguard him during his most vulnerable period. Routine visits to your veterinarian are also recommended, especially while the puppy is under one year of age. The vet may notice something that did not seem important to you.

EYES
Large, expressive, soft

HEAD
Proportioned

TEETH
Strong, meet in scissor bite

EARS
Medium sized, hanging, covered with hair

NECK
Strong, slightly arched

FOREQUARTERS
Laid back

Westminster Kennel Club 1995 Best of Breed winner Ch. Diotima Bear Necessity, owned by Pat McDonald and Karen Kaye